HE CHANGED THEM

Their Moment of Truth

HE CHANGED THEM

David Porter

Christian Focus Publications

For Peter and Pam Cousins

'Musick in the House, Musick in the Heart, and Musick also in Heaven, for joy that we are here.'

John Bunyan, *The Pilgrim's Progress*, Part II

© 1995 David Porter
ISBN 1-85792-038-4

Published by
Christian Focus Publications Ltd
Geanies House, Fearn, Ross-shire,
IV20 1TW, Scotland, Great Britain.

Cover design by Donna Macleod

Printed and bound in Great Britain by
Cox & Wyman Ltd, Reading, Berkshire.

Contents

Preface

The chapters that follow tell of episodes in the lives of ten Christians from the beginnings of the Christian church (Augustine) to the present day (Laszlo Tokes).

But they are not intended to be 'potted biographies'. Instead, each chapter focuses on a particular event, sequence of events or period in its subject's life which in some way deeply affected their future or proved to be the point to which their previous life had been leading. For some, these moments were those for which they have always been remembered (for example, the conversion of John Wesley); for others, they are times of taking stock and striking out in different directions (for example, David Livingstone's furlough in Britain); and in still others, they are periods or events in their subject's life that may not have had much attention paid to them but were in fact extremely significant (for example, Jim Elliot's student years at Wheaton College).

I have provided for each chapter notes for further reading and information about sites and memorials associated with its subject. Because much of the writing of this book has involved difficult decisions about what to leave out, I have included in the notes full details of at least one standard biography for each chapter.

1

The Conversion of St Augustine

Like a Colossus bestriding two worlds, Augustine stands as the last patristic and the first mediaeval father of Western Christianity .... He was no mere eclectic. The centre of his 'system' is the Holy Scriptures, as they ordered and moved his heart and mind. It was in Scripture that, first and last, Augustine found the focus of his religious authority.[1]

Augustine was born in AD 354 in the African town of Tagaste, which today is Souk-Ahras in modern Algeria. When he was born the town was three centuries old, part of the Roman empire's showpiece border-territory of Numidia; intensively cultivated and well supplied with roads and towns, the region was very different to what it is today. There was hunting and good living, and olive forests covered the slopes, though Numidia had no great benefit from the luxuries she produced. They were exported or taken to Rome at prices which were all in Rome's favour. Tagaste was under the local rule of Carthage on the Mediterranean coast, but was 2,000 feet above sea level and 200 miles from the sea. The region had been romanised in a very short time:

In Africa urbanization proceeded rapidly, based in the province's eastern regions on the existing Punic communities and in Numidia on the development of native settlements, supplemented as always by Roman colonies.[2]

Roman Africa produced many lawyers and celebrated writers, and received Christianity at an early date. 'The churches in the area were the first Latin-speaking churches of the world. It is probable that the first translations of the Scriptures into Latin were made in North Africa.'[3] The North African church had a highly organised system of bishoprics and provincial councils, and before Augustine rose to prominence it had already produced at least two of the great Fathers of the church, Tertullian (c. 160-220) and Cyprian (d. 258).

Augustine's homeland was a farming region. His family, though poor, were Roman citizens. His father Patricius was a pagan, his mother Monica a Christian. They gave up much to ensure that Augustine received an education; it was a way out of the hinterland, a passport to position and income. Within his family Augustine was privileged, for his cousins had no education at all. In his spiritual autobiography, *The Confessions*, he recalls that he 'had no love of learning, and hated to be driven to it'. He disliked Greek literature, but loved the Latin writers.

Monica was a faithful believer. She may have been a member of the Berber people, who still live in North Africa. If so, her background would have predisposed her to some extent to Christianity. The Berbers lived in Palestine centuries before Christ, and spread through Asia Minor and Southern Europe, eventually settling in Africa. Never conquered by the Arabs (today they still resist Arabisation), they accepted Muhammad as religious leader, but refused to bow to Qu'ranic law. Similarly their kinsmen the Numidians had declined to accept the gods and goddesses of Greece and Rome, preferring their own 'high gods', of whom the greatest was Saturn. They retained their identity under Roman rule – the 'Berber' or 'Libyan' language is mentioned frequently in contemporary writings, and its survival in the early African Church may have been an underlying factor in several of the historic conflicts – and were prominent in the early centuries of the Christian church. Though a proud and independent race, disdainful of imposed laws, many Berbers became Christians and formed the backbone of the African church.

African religion was often bizarre and many of its practices were imitated or observed by local Christians. There was a pagan deity said to dwell in Carthage, for example, whose presence was announced by a huge statue to which many Christians along with the pagans dedicated their children. An awareness of the supernatural and a respect for dreams and visions pervaded both Christian and pagan communities.

Monica was brought up in a Christian home, and when old enough was given in marriage to Patricius: whereupon, Augustine confesses,

> She busied herself to gain him unto thee [God], preaching thee to him by her behaviour, in which thou madest her fair and reverently amiable, and admirable to her husband. For she endured with patience his infidelity and never had any dissension with her husband on this account. For she waited for thy mercy upon him until, by believing in thee, he might become chaste.[4]

Not surprisingly, Augustine records that there were tensions in the marriage, though Monica was a strong woman and coped well with her husband's overbearing demands and his infidelities. Though she nominally acknowledged the subordination of women to their husbands, and their status as virtual chattels, she quietly pursued her own agenda both as wife and mother.

When she was twenty-three, she gave birth to Augustine, and a mother-son relationship began which was to become one of the wonders of Christian testimony. In his spiritual autobiography, the *Confessions*, that relationship is spelt out in great detail, though Augustine is as frequently critical of his father as he is adoring of his mother:

> When my father saw me one day at the baths and perceived that I was becoming a man, and was

showing the signs of adolescence, he joyfully told
my mother about it as if already looking forward to
grandchildren, rejoicing in that sort of inebriation in
which the world so often forgets thee, its Creator, and
falls in love with thy creature instead of thee – the
inebriation of that invisible wine of a perverted will
which turns and bows down to infamy. But in my
mother's breast thou hadst already begun to build thy
temple and the foundation of thy holy habitation ...[5]

Both his father and mother, however, were determined that their son should receive a good education.

I had come back from Madaura, a neighbouring city
where I had gone to study grammar and rhetoric; and
the money for a further term at Carthage was being
got together for me. This project was more a matter
of my father's ambition than of his means, for he was
only a poor citizen of Tagaste.[6]

Madaura was a university city of cultured pagans,
but Carthage university was more renowned, more
prestigious and more expensive. It took Patricius a
year to accumulate the necessary money for the
fees. It was not a happy year for Augustine. In a part
of the *Confessions* which demonstrates why Augustine is regarded as a master of psychological
observation, he describes the torments of sexual
awakening, the 'thornbushes of lust', and his mother's sage counsel against fornication and adultery.
   Looking back years later, he recognised Monica's words as words from God. But he rejected

them at the time, and plunged into a hectic life of immorality, competing with his friends to prove that he could be every bit as worldly as they were.

> I made myself out worse than I was, in order that I might not go lacking for praise. And when in any-thing I had not sinned as the worst ones in the group, I would still say that I had done what I had not done, in order not to appear contemptible because I was more innocent than they; and not to drop in their esteem because I was more chaste.[7]

His mother, he noted, made no concessions to her son's physical maturity of which her husband had gleefully told her. It was chastity she urged her son to follow, not adolescent experimentation. But nei-ther did she believe that marriage was necessarily the way to sublimate his desires; a wife might well stand in the way of his hopes of a good education. It was not the prestige and glory of the scholar's life that Monica wanted for her son, he records, but the opportunity, in the quiet reflection of the academic life, for her turbulent son to return to God. In an extraordinary gamble by Monica, 'the reins of discipline were slackened on me', and Augustine plunged further into recklessness.

Few people have analysed their own pre-con-version lostness as acutely as Augustine did in the *Confessions*. John Bunyan came near it in the document his church required of new members (a document known to us today as *Grace Abounding to the Chief of Sinners*) but it is very vulnerable to the charge of being a formula-piece, its exaggeration diminishing realism and candour. Bunyan's self-analysis is nowhere near as complex and perceptive as that which he brought to bear on his most famous creations, the characters of *The Pilgrim's Progress*. Augustine, however, is brilliantly unsparing of his own moral failings.

'It was foul, and I loved it,' he writes. 'I loved my error – not that for which I erred, but the error itself.'[8] He stole 'a huge load of pears', but once he had them in his possession he barely bothered to taste them before getting rid of them to a herd of pigs. It was not the pears he was interested in. 'What was it in you, O theft of mine,' he ponders, 'that I, poor wretch, doted on you – you deed of darkness – in the sixteenth year of my age?' And why, he reflects, was it so important that he should have joined with others in the theft, rather than stealing the pears on his own? 'O friendship all unfriendly!'

Contemplating his wild exploits of his sixteenth year, the future saint despaired of understanding what had prompted them. 'Who can unravel such a twisted and tangled knottiness?' He hated to think of it, and he thirsted for righteousness and innocence; but that was in later years, when he sat down to write the *Confessions*. The teenage Augustine had no such thoughts.

I fell away from thee, O my God, and in my youth I

wandered too far from thee, my true support. And I
became to myself a wasteland.[9]

When at the age of seventeen Augustine finally
arrived in Carthage he was, he says, 'not in love as
yet, but I was in love with love'. He was looking for
something to love so that his hunger for the experience of loving could be satisfied. He was unaware
of the spiritual emptiness within himself, and de-
spised the spiritual food – God himself – who
would have filled it: 'The emptier I became the
more I loathed [that food]'.[10] In his poem 'The
Waste Land' (1922), T. S. Eliot used Augustine's
arrival in the great city as an image of twentieth-
century alienation, quoting in his notes Augustine's comment 'To Carthage then I came, where a
cauldron of unholy loves sang all about mine ears.'[11]

At Carthage there were plentiful opportunities
for the young student to indulge himself. He discovered the theatre, and found in sad plays a kind of
inverted pleasure. He was especially fond of plays
that portrayed people in love, particularly if the
drama involved a tragic separation. Just as he had
been a young man looking for something to love, so
he was now a young man looking for things over
which to grieve. Later he was to recognise that the
appeal of other people's grief, even fictional grief,
had been that it was a superficial, second-hand
sorrow that left his own inner turmoil largely undis-
turbed – 'the sort of grief which came from hearing
those fictions, which affected only the surface of

my emotion.' And yet, he adds, his griefs did have
a deeper effect: 'just as if they had been poisoned
fingernails, their scratching was followed by in-
flammation, swelling, putrefaction and corruption.
Such was my life! But was it life, O my God?'[12]

Youthful wildness was comparatively short-
lived. By the time Augustine was nineteen his
father had died, and Monica had taken on the
burden of paying for her son's education.[13] He was
far from settling down, though he was soon to take
a mistress to whom he remained attached for fifteen
years, and to father a son. He added the Scriptures
to his academic interests but judged them to be
inferior to his favourite Latin authors; he admired
those in Carthage who discussed theology cleverly
and learnedly but without spiritual discernment.
Though he had not severed his links with the
Carthage church, he joined in the laughter when
God was ridiculed, and applauded those who rejected orthodox Christianity in favour of idiosyncratic versions of the faith.

One school of thought attracted him particularly. As an older man he marvelled that he had known
how to reject the fables of Roman mythology, yet
had accepted so easily the teaching of the Manichaeans. Manes, the founder, was a Persian who
began teaching around AD 240 and was driven into
exile in India by opposition from the Zoroastrians.
Later he returned home but was executed by a
former protector; his followers were banished.

Manichaeism, which resembles Zoroastrianism in several details, taught that there was an age-old conflict between light and darkness. Religion's function was to release the imprisoned light that was in human brains, and Jesus, Buddha and other prophets had come to the world to help mankind in that task. The Manichaean scriptures were poetic and mystical. Manichaeans practised a severely austere lifestyle and ate no meat; devotees rose through a system of ascetic grades. The new religion spread rapidly, and was widely taught in Africa, though it was regarded with suspicion and was illegal in Carthage.

Augustine's later recollections of the teaching (and of his own acceptance of it) were scathing:

> How much better were the fables of the grammarians and poets than these snares! .... Woe, woe, by what steps I was dragged down to 'the depths of hell' — toiling and fuming because of my lack of the truth, even when I was seeking after thee, my God! .... For I was ignorant of that other reality, true Being. And so it was that I was subtly persuaded to agree with these foolish deceivers when they put their questions to me ....[14]

In 373, he came across a book by Cicero, *The Hortensius*, which is now lost. Augustine had planned to be a lawyer, but had turned to study literature and rhetoric, of which he became a teacher. Cicero was a master of Latin style, and Augustine was drawn to books of eloquence. *The Hortensius,* a commendation of philosophy, 'quite definitely changed my whole attitude and turned my prayers toward thee, O Lord, and gave me new hope and new desires.'

Cicero's exhortation to wisdom seized Augustine's imagination so that he longed to obtain wisdom for himself, rather than to follow self-seeking teachers or fragmenting sects. Acutely, he notes that despite this his enthusiasm had limits:

> Only this checked my ardour: that the name of Christ was not in it. For this name, by thy mercy, O Lord, this name of my Saviour thy Son, my tender heart had piously drunk in, deeply treasured even with my mother's milk. And whatsoever was lacking that name, no matter how erudite, polished, and truthful, did not quite take complete hold of me.[15]

Peter Brown has suggested that 'Augustine was a boy from a Christian household .... Paganism meant nothing to Augustine.'[16] That was why a pagan wisdom outside the Bible held no real attraction for him. The name of Christ, like baptism, was a guarantee of safety.

Augustine turned to the Bible to look for the kind of wisdom he wanted, but did not find what he was seeking. He turned next to the Manichaeans. And at the very beginning of his involvement, he considers in the *Confessions*, God was already making provision for him to find the truth. Why else, he asks, should Monica have suddenly had an extraordinary dream?

She had seen herself standing weeping, bowed down with sorrow. A 'bright youth' had approached her, happy and smiling, and asked her why she was in such distress. She had told him that she was grieving over the doom of her son's soul. He told her to be happy; where she was, there was her son too. And Monica had looked up, and there was Augustine standing with her in the same place.

When she told her son what she had seen in her dream he volunteered the strikingly unimaginative interpretation that she should not despair of some day achieving what he himself had achieved. But she replied immediately that the meaning of the dream was the opposite; that he would one day be where *she* was.

It was a gift from God for Monica, a 'consolation for her present anguish' and a response to her piety and prayers for her wayward son. It was not the only gift. She asked a learned bishop if he would talk to her son and convince him of his errors; the bishop declined, on the grounds that Augustine was in no mood to listen to good advice. 'Just pray for him,' he advised. 'He will see the error of the Manichaeans on his own, as he reads and considers.' It had happened in exactly that way, he told her, in his own experience.

The advice tallied perfectly with Monica's own

reasons for wanting her son educated, but she found the bishop's advice hard to take and pleaded with him tearfully to talk to Augustine. Eventually he became irritated. 'Be off with you! How could the son of tears like that possibly perish?' Monica happily accepted the words as a message from God.[17]

However, nine long years were to pass before Augustine would fully turn to God. They were to be nine years spent as a Manichaean, during which he taught rhetoric in public, took a mistress whose name he does not reveal, and promoted the Manichaean heresy enthusiastically. He was a spiritual elitist, and hated the sacrifices and rituals of the pagans, though he was not averse to consulting astrologers because they had no sacrifice rituals. When a close godly friend almost died and was baptised without knowing it, Augustine tried to make light of the baptism when the friend recovered. The friend rebuked him, and Augustine decided to wait until recovery was complete before ridding him of his religious nonsense. But the friend soon died, and with him died one check on Augustine's spiritual decline. For months afterwards, he was obsessed with thoughts of death.

MANICHAEISM had an understandable attraction for somebody whose mind was as acute as Augustine's was. It gave that mind freedom without encumber-

ing it with the trappings of traditional Christianity,
and promised a vital, immediate experience of
God.

> The Manichee did not need to be ordered to believe.
> He could grasp, for himself, the essence of religion.
> Immediacy was what mattered most. The crucifixion
> of Christ spoke directly to such a man of the suffer-
> ings of his own soul. His hero was Doubting Tho-
> mas, a man whose yearning for a direct, immediate
> contact with the divine secrets had not been spurned
> by Christ.[18]

Many of the teachings of the Manichaeans, so
admired by the young Augustine, later became
targets of his prolific theological writings. Disillu-
sionment in fact set in quite early, as the young
Augustine chafed at the limitations of a system that
concentrated on the present moment and ignored
both doubts and uncertainties, and the desire to
grow spiritually and explore more deeply.

It was a visitor to Carthage in AD 383 who
provoked Augustine, at the age of twenty-nine, to
reject Manichaeism – Faustus, a Manichaean bishop, 'a great snare of the devil'. As Augustine
listened to Faustus' skilled eloquence he realised
that quality of presentation was not the same as
quality of content. He had looked forward 'with
unbounded eagerness' to meeting the visiting scholar: 'But what profit was there to me in the elegance
of my cupbearer, since he could not offer me the

more precious draught for which I thirsted?'[19]

He found that he was not allowed to ask the questions that troubled him, and when he seized the chance to talk to Faustus in private he rapidly decided that 'Faustus was ignorant in those arts in which I had believed him eminent'. It was enough to pour cold water on his zeal for Manichaeism. He turned to study literature with the bishop, but, as he wrote afterwards, 'all my endeavours to make further progress in Manichaeism came completely to an end through my acquaintance with that man.'

THE Carthaginian student body was wild and undisciplined, which had not troubled Augustine as a student but was becoming wearisome to him as a teacher. It was the prospect of quiet lecture halls, more than that of a higher income and more prestigious appointment, that drew him to Rome, where he opened a school of rhetoric. By then his formal links with Manichaeism were severed, though by inclination he remained a Manichaean in many matters.

In Rome he became seriously ill. Far away, Monica, unaware of her son's physical plight, prayed, as she had always done, for the salvation of his soul. She was, in Augustine's words, 'pure and prudent ... constant in her alms, gracious and attentive to thy saints, never missing a visit to church twice a day, morning and evening ... in order that she might listen to thee in thy sermons, and thou to her in her prayers'.[20]

He recovered, and began to toy with the teaching of the 'Academics', who taught that absolute truth could never be gained. He gained pupils, who came to him in his home for teaching, and were just as well-behaved as he had been told they were. But he was appalled to find it a common practice for students to change teachers without warning, to avoid paying their fees. This treachery upset him much more than the immoral lives many led in Rome, and when a post fell vacant for a teacher of rhetoric in Milan he lost no time in applying; he was successful, and arrived there in AD 384. In Milan he met one of the great influences on his life, Bishop Ambrose.

> That man of God received me as a father would, and welcomed my coming as a good bishop should. And I began to love him, of course, not at the first as a teacher of the truth, for I had entirely despaired of finding that in thy Church – but as a friendly man.[21]

It was in Ambrose that he found the combination he desired, of beautiful oratory and sound teaching. He discovered that the Christian faith could, after all, be amply defended against the Manichaean heresy. He was not yet a Christian, but he rejected Manichaeism 'even in that period of doubt', believing that the philosophers had more of the truth.

The foundations laid by his Christian mother,

and (as he gladly recognised) her devoted prayer for him over the years, began to bear fruit. He became a catechumen (somebody receiving instruction prior to baptism) in the Milan church; which in itself was not remarkable, as Monica was planning a marriage for him to a wealthy Catholic woman and church membership was a strategic move.

Monica arrived in Milan in AD 385. She too fell under the spell of Ambrose. Augustine continued to attend church with her, and began to delight in reading the Bible. Yet he still hung back, 'just as it happens that a man who has tried a bad physician fears to trust himself with a good one'. It was faith that Augustine needed, not more learning. Without it, the old Augustine still flourished: eager, enquiring, proud and ambitious, ruthlessly stripping away falsehood but reluctant to embrace the divine love that had never let him go.

His view of God at this time was as 'some kind of a body in space, either infused into the world, or infinitely diffused beyond the world'[22]. By clever reasoning he managed to explain God out of the way, and moved on to wrestle with the question of the origin of evil. Yet in the middle of his philosophical musings he never discarded the fact that he was responsible for his own sin, rather than being the tool of some higher force. In the *Confessions* he records a step-by-step progress to the concept of a good God who is not the author of evil. All this was

going on while 'still the faith of thy Christ, our Lord
and Saviour, as it was taught me by the Catholic
church, stuck fast in my heart. As yet it was unformed
on many points and diverged from the rule of right
doctrine, but my mind did not utterly lose it, and
every day drank in more and more of it.'[23]

By AD 386, Augustine had become a neo-Platonist, the last step in his long journey of the mind
towards Christianity. Neo-Platonism taught that in
the One who was behind all experience, dualism
could be overcome and life be placed on a rational
and intellectually satisfying basis. But in 386 he
went to see Simplicianus, Ambrose's spiritual director, and heard the story of the neo-Platonist
Victorinus, who had become a Christian after a life
of academic celebrity and devoted neo-Platonism.
Augustine was thrilled by the story but recognised
that the biggest obstacle in his own path was 'the
iron chain' of his will, and the carnality that came
from it.

> My two wills – the old and the new, the carnal and the
> spiritual – were in conflict within me; and by their
> discord they tore my soul apart.[24]

He was, he says, like a man slumbering and struggling to wake up:

> On all sides, thou didst show me that thy words are
> true and I, convicted by the truth, had nothing at all
> to reply but the drawling and drowsy words: 'Pres-
> ently ...'[25]

A Christian visiting Augustine and his friend Alypius was delighted to find Paul's writings there. While they were talking together Augustine was overwhelmed by his own spiritual ugliness and folly in preferring sensual delights to the things of God. How often he had prayed, 'Make me chaste, Lord – but not yet ...'! Tormented by his inner struggles, he went into the garden; Alypius followed anxiously, and watched Augustine's frenzied gestures. How strange it is, Augustine later commented, that the mind so easily commands the body yet resists its own commands to itself.

He mentally reviewed the intellectual and spiritual roads he had travelled, 'reproaching myself more bitterly than ever, rolling and writhing in my chain until it should be utterly broken.'[26] In the *Confessions* he portrays the struggle graphically, addressing, as he always does, his sins and failings directly by name and describing his follies as seductive deceiving charmers who 'tugged at my fleshly garments'. And as Alypius 'awaited in silence the outcome of my extraordinary agitation', Chastity herself appeared to Augustine in a vision: 'Cast yourself on [God] without fear, for he will receive and heal you.'

He needed to be completely alone. He went to another part of the garden, leaving behind Alypius and the copy of the Epistle to the Romans which he had taken into the garden with him. Flinging himself down under a fig tree he wept uncontrollably,

pleading with God to take away his sin: 'Why not
now? Why not this very hour make an end to my
uncleanness?'

And then he heard the voice of a child.

The words of an infant's song in a neighbouring
garden wove themselves through his tears. 'Pick it
up, read it, pick it up, read it.' He stopped weeping,
asking himself whether he had ever heard such a
song before. He knew he had not. Immediately he
recognised the words as a command from God. He
must go back, and, just as he knew others had done
before him, he must open the Bible and read whatever he saw there.

Alypius, who had considerately not pursued his
friend and in any case was having spiritual turmoils
of his own, must have been surprised to see Augustine reappear, dry-eyed, and snatch the Epistle to
the Romans from the bench where it lay.

In silence [I] read the paragraph on which my eyes
first fell: 'Not in rioting and drunkenness, not in
chambering and wantonness, not in strife and envy-
ing, but put on the Lord Jesus Christ, and make no
provision for the flesh to fulfil the lusts thereof.' I
wanted to read no further, nor did I need to. For
instantly, as the sentence ended, there was infused in
my heart something like the light of full certainty and
all the gloom of doubt vanished away.[27]

His face marked by a new tranquillity, he told
Alypius what had happened, and Alypius, who

though not tormented like Augustine with carnal desires was spiritually hungry too, joined him 'in full commitment without any hesitation'.

Monica was indoors. Perhaps she had an inkling what was going on; perhaps she had been praying for Augustine during his spiritual crisis in the garden. We do not know. Certainly she was used to her son's spiritual agonies; she must have often prayed for him in one room while he wept in another.

We do know, for Augustine tells us so, that when the two men came to tell her what had happened she 'leaped for joy triumphant'. For 'she saw that thou didst so convert me to thee that I sought neither a wife nor any other of this world's hopes, but set my feet on that rule of faith which so many years before thou hadst showed her in her dream about me. And so thou didst turn her grief into gladness more plentiful than she had ventured to desire and dearer and purer than the desire she used to cherish of having grandchildren of my flesh.'[28]

THAT is the point at which Augustine's tale, in the *Confessions*, is told. There is one final, though not insignificant, autobiographical chapter in which he describes how he resigned his professorship and was baptised into the Christian church. He went back to Africa with Monica, where they lived in great happiness at Ostia, and where they shared a spiritual experience of intense ecstasy. Shortly afterwards Monica contracted a fever and died. Augustine wrote movingly of her pious death, and closed his spiritual autobiography (the first nine books or chapters of the *Confessions*) with profound gratitude for Monica, Patricius, and all those who with them are citizens of the New Jerusalem.

Notes

1. Albert C. Outler (trs and ed), *Augustine: Confessions and Enchiridion* (SCM, 1955), p 13.
2. Tim Cornell and John Matthews, *Atlas of the Roman World* (Adromeda/Equinox 1991), p 28.
3. Stephen Neill, *A History of Christian Missions* (Penguin, 1964), p 37.
4. *Confessions* IX.9: Outler p 190.
5. *Confessions* II.3: Outler p 53.
6. *Ibid*: Outler p 52.
7. *Ibid*: Outler p 53.
8. *Confessions*, II.4: Outler p 55.
9. *Confessions*, II.10: Outler p 60.
10. *Confessions*, III.1: Outler p 61.
11. T. S. Eliot, 'The Waste Land' (1922), notes to part IV.
12. *Confessions*, III.2: Outler p.63.
13. *Confessions*, III.4: Outler p 65. It is noticeable that Augustine mentions his father's death almost inconsequentially, by contrast with the way he describes Monica's death later.
14. *Confessions*, III.6,7: Outler p 68.
15. *Confessions*, III.4: Outler p 65.
16. Peter Brown, *Augustine of Hippo* (Faber & Faber, 1967), p 41.
17. *Confessions*, III.12: Outler p 75.
18. Peter Brown, *op cit*, p 49.
19. *Confessions*, V.6: Outler p 101.
20. *Confessions*, V.10: Outler p 106.
21. *Confessions*, V.13: Outler p 110.

22. *Confessions,* VII.1: Outler p 135.
23. *Confessions*, VII. 5: Outler p 140.
24. *Confessions*, VIII.5: Outler p 164.
25. *Confessions*, *ibid*: Outler p 165.
26. *Confessions,* VIII.11: Outler p 173.
27. *Confessions*, VIII.12: Outler p 175.
28. *Confessions*, *ibid*: Outler p 177.

2

Martin Luther
The Nailing of the Ninety-Five Theses

One of the great ironies of the European Reformation is that the immense public interest aroused by Martin Luther's 'Ninety-Five Theses' probably surprised nobody more than Luther himself. The act of posting these propositions for debate on the door of the Castle Church in Wittenberg on 31 October 1517 – an act that has for centuries been recognised as the decisive initiation of the Reformation – was never intended to provoke a public outcry. The language in which the Theses were written demonstrates as much; they were in Latin, the language of academic discourse, and their author, Professor Martin Luther, was setting them before the academics who attended the church as matters for urgent theological discussion.

It has often been pointed out that had Luther set out to create Protestantism, he would have found very little support. But his purpose was, literally, to reform the church as he knew it. 'Though he promoted a rebellion,' wrote H. A. L. Fisher, 'he was not a revolutionary.'[1] Owen Chadwick remarks, 'He intended no revolution, he aimed at purifying the Catholic Church and preserving its truth.'[2] In

Martin Luther and the Birth of Protestantism, James Atkinson writes, 'He was simply a man with a Gospel ... Luther was thrust into the tumult of the Reformation and never sought it.'[3] James M. Kittelson, his modern biographer, concludes: 'He tried mightily to be loyal to Rome, and then condemned Rome utterly.'[4]

The nailing of the Ninety-Five Theses was typical of Luther's agenda. It was not an attempt to bring down the church. It was a protest against a huge abuse of ecclesiastical authority: the sale of indulgences.

LUTHER's life by 1517 had already been eventful. Born in Eisleben in 1483 the son of a prosperous miner, at the age of fourteen he was taught at a school in Magdeburg run by a mystical lay movement, the Brethren of the Common Life, which though not a recognised monastic order required its members to take informal Vows. Among others who were members or pupils were Erasmus and Thomas à Kempis. At Magdeburg he supplemented his income by singing, developing an interest in music that continued when in 1498 he was sent to continue his education at Eisenach – where, in 1685, the great composer J. S. Bach would be born and attend the same school. After three especially happy years there, he was sent by his father in 1501 to university in Erfurt to study theology. At this point in his life he was not particularly religious; he followed the teachings of the Catholic Church, attended Confession with all its rigorous searching, and duly observed the heavy penances that the priests imposed.

Life in a mediaeval university was, like mediaeval religion, hard work. The university at Erfurt was not like a modern campus, but was a small collection of buildings resembling a monastery in appearance and organisation. The emphasis was on a disciplined life and on tuition by scholars, typically conducted by means of 'disputations' or public debates. Martin was a brilliant student, completing his studies comfortably within the prescribed time and acquiring – perhaps for his skill in debate – the nickname 'The Philosopher' and a reputation for being a cheerful, hard-working student.

He was awarded the Bachelor of Arts degree in 1502, for studies in grammar, dialectic and rhetoric; continuing with studies in music, arithmetic, geometry, astronomy and philosophy he gained his Master's degree in 1505. It was a period of academic ferment. The Renaissance, which had begun in Italy in the fourteenth century as a revival of interest in the culture and art of the classics, had begun to spread north, and in the process had acquired a religious dimension that had been somewhat lacking in Renaissance humanist Italy: scholars such as Thomas More and John Colet in England and Erasmus in Switzerland – part of a tradition known as 'Christian Humanism' – turned their attention to the apostolic and other early church texts, where their southern counterparts had explored the pagan classics. The Christian humanists were so called because they wanted to apply what they had found to the church to which they belonged, and over the fourteenth and fifteenth centuries the Roman Catholic leadership experienced the impact of Renaissance thinking in many ways.

And so Martin Luther became a student at a time when the European world of learning was passing through one of the great seminal changes in the history of ideas; and he began his long confrontation with the church at a time when the hierarchy had already been exposed to challenge. It is often argued that Luther was harvesting work already begun by such people as Erasmus. Certainly the impact of the Renaissance on recent popes had been to consolidate a hierarchy that had become fascinated by material splendour and less interested in feeding the souls of its flock. Of Pope Alexander VI it was said, 'His election [in 1492] was owing partly to the disputes that arose between two cardinals ... but chiefly to a simony [buying and selling of jobs in the church] unheard of in those days'. When in 1511 Pope Julius II took it upon himself to lead a besieging army against the French, it was said: 'It was certainly a remarkable case ... to behold the High Priest, the Vicar of Christ on earth, old and infirm, and educated in ease and pleasures, now employed in person in managing a war excited by himself against Christians ...'[5]

One enduring symbol of the Renaissance's contribution to the Church of Rome is the mighty edifice of the church of St Peter in Rome. It will always be associated with Pope Leo X, the son of Lorenzo the Magnificent, who took holy orders, was consecrated bishop and was crowned pope all in the space of four days in March 1513. Leo's love of the arts was in direct contrast to the bellicose Julius II – one reason, in fact, for his election. Forced to think continually of new ways of funding his prolific spending on the arts, he commissioned the sale of indulgences to pay for the building of St Peter's. As indulgences were the abuse against which Luther's outrage was first directed, Leo can be fairly described as being the cause of the Reformation – though he may well have been more pious than some of his predecessors, and he seems to have loved the arts for their own sake rather than out of ostentation or arrogance.

EARLY in 1505 Luther received his Master's degree, an occasion which he regarded as the height of worldly happiness and which made his father justly proud of him: the professions were now open to Martin and also the prospect of wealth and position; the law and future government office were within his reach. But in July of the same year Hans

Luther's enjoyment of his son's new dignity was shattered by the news that Martin, flung to the ground by a bolt of lightning while out walking, had vowed to St Anne that he would become a monk if his life were spared.

Probably the thunderstorm experience was the culmination of long and agonised pondering about his future – after all, he had just finished several years of education. He may well have discussed with his teachers and his family the possibility of entering a monastery. Even so, the announcement that Martin had exchanged a prosperous future for one to be spent under vows of poverty was a bitter blow, and Hans Luther told his son so. Martin's reply was that he was convinced that the bolt of lightning had been God's direct word to him. It says much for Hans Luther's pragmatic piety that he came to accept his son's conviction. By September Martin had given away all his possessions and become a member of the Order of Observant Augustinians in Erfurt, and by summer 1506 had become a friar there.

The Augustinians were prominent in Erfurt. The Order, established in 1243, now had over 2,000 chapters and had a reputation for discipline that must have attracted Luther, who embarked on fasting, lowly domestic duties and ascetic contemplation with enthusiasm. He was a rigorous follower of an austere monastic path, faithfully following the Order's rule and studying the Bible painstakingly. His main work was theology, but he was given administrative responsibilities as well. He spent his time lecturing, writing up his lectures, reading to the monks at mealtimes, writing letters and carrying out many other duties as well as the normal ones of a monk. In 1507, after remarkably rapid progress, he became a priest and celebrated his first Mass, which was attended by his family. At the banquet that followed, an uneasy conversation between Hans and Martin showed that Hans was still not entirely reconciled to his son's vocation.

Martin Luther himself, though he did not regret obeying the call to the priesthood, was troubled by the harsh ascetic regime which may well have contributed to the medical problems that plagued him throughout his life, and by the practice of confession, which in the monastery was a deep psychological probing which precipitated anguished self-doubts – probably made worse by the physical stress of the monk's life. It was in these years that he became attracted to the writings of Paul, in whose teachings he sensed the possibility of resolving his spiritual torment:

> Though an impeccable friar, I stood before God as a sinner troubled in conscience, and I had no confidence that my merit would assuage him. Therefore I did not love a just and angry God, but rather hated and murmured against him. Yet I clung to the dear Paul and had a great yearning to know what he meant.[6]

He was making his mark as a theologian and a scholar; in the winter of 1508 he lectured for a term at Wittenberg University: only recently established, the university was short of teachers. Luther lectured on Aristotle, and before a year had passed was back in Erfurt.

Internal politics in the Augustinian Order caused ripples which resulted in a meeting at Nuremberg: a proposed unification of all the Augustinian houses had brought protests from the stricter establishments, who feared that their monks would be allowed to become slack and easy-going under the influence of less rigorous houses. Luther went to Nuremberg as companion to the Erfurt delegates. Dissatisfied with the outcome, the Erfurt monks set out to walk to Rome to argue their case there. Though they had little success, the experience of going to Rome was a memorable one for Luther. Deeply committed to the significance of the church's institutions and authority (which is why he was so outraged when that authority was abused), he gloried in the masses and pageantry, which symbolised for him the reality of the Holy City in which the pope ruled as Christ's earthly regent. Yet he was not blind to the wealth and splendour in which the hierarchy lived: in later life he claimed to be very glad to have seen Rome for himself, as otherwise he might have wondered whether he had been rather too hard on the pope.

The crisis at Erfurt split the monastery. Luther

decided that his responsibility was to submit to the authority of the Augustinians at Wittenberg; in 1511 he transferred to the Augustinian House there, where he was under the authority of Johann von Staupitz, twenty years his senior, who would become a trusted friend and counsellor. Shortly afterwards he entered Wittenberg University, earning his doctorate of theology in 1512. At the age of 29 he became Professor of Holy Scripture.

It took considerable persuasion and a good deal of pulling rank on Staupitz's part before Luther was willing to consider becoming a professor. He conceded later that neither doctorate nor professorship were of his own choosing, but were acts of pious obedience. Few monks were chosen to make the transition from the theological studies of the monastery to the academic cut-and-thrust of the university; but Luther was, which indicates the regard in which Staupitz and his other superiors held him.

Theological scholarship of the period was absorbed with the question of the absolute holiness of God. Though often propounded aridly and discussed as an abstraction, for Martin the issue was a profoundly personal one which threw into sharp relief his awareness of the sin of humanity and his own in particular. It was a remorseless self-searching for which the years of frequent confession in Erfurt had prepared him. Looking back on those years he observed,

> Though I lived as a monk without reproach, I felt that I was a sinner before God with an extremely disturbed conscience. I could not believe that he was placated by my satisfaction. I did not love, yes, I hated the righteous God who punishes sinners, and secretly, if not blasphemously, certainly murmuring greatly, I was angry with God, and said, 'As if, indeed, that it is not enough, that miserable sinners, eternally lost through original sin, are crushed by every kind of calamity by the law of the Decalogue, without having God add pain to pain by the gospel and also by the gospel threatening us with his righteousness and wrath!' [7]

After a typically arduous bout of spiritual exercises, he wondered, 'Who knows whether these things please God?' He recorded his spiritual uncertainty:

> It is God's eternity, holiness and power which thus continually threaten man throughout the whole of his life ... God's ever-present judgement clutches man in the loneliness of his conscience, and with his every breath conveys him to the Almighty and Holy One to prosper or destroy.[8]

Luther's expositions of theology drew on his remarkable knowledge of the Bible: in 1513 he began lecturing on the Psalms, in 1515 on Romans, in 1516 on Galatians, and in 1517 on Hebrews.

It was a time of great excitement for Luther, who as he prepared and delivered his lectures found an intellectual landscape opening up to him that stood in opposition to the renaissance landscape in which he had been educated; he drew heavily from the Church Fathers in preference to the classical writers of antiquity. 'Aristotle is gradually declining,' he marvelled, as he began to recognise the Bible as relevant, authoritative and intellectually credible into the bargain. The texts of his lectures survive, and they reveal a growing scepticism towards the notion of earned merit and the beginnings of a doctrine of undeserved grace. In 1516 he spoke in a public debate at Wittenberg where he found himself arguing against the prevailing *via moderna*, the argument that God, being all-powerful and entirely holy, must be placated by sinful human beings if they were ever to have dealings with him. Thus far, even the mature Luther would have assented. But the academics of the *via moderna* argued that human love, human repentance and human faith were all weak and inadequate. Although God was a God of grace (they agreed, with St Paul), only the mediation of the church of Christ could ensure that one's salvation was sure.

From this starting point, the doctrine of salvation by works, earned merit and ecclesiastical absolution developed. The young Luther accepted it unquestioningly: it was a coherent and intellectually satisfying scheme, though it plunged his soul into dismay. He embarked on his monastic career determined to discipline his life and his soul in order to guarantee his standing before God. By the time of the debate of 1516, however, he was seeing things differently.

The change was a slow one, traceable, in many of its details, in those of his sermons and lectures which survive. He was encouraged by Staupitz, who talked often to him about God's grace, of penitence, of loving righteousness and loving God. But Luther's problem was that he knew all about grace. He knew about the absolution that lay within the power of the priest; he knew that the church possessed a store of grace that could be credited to him were he only to obey the ordinances of the church and demonstrate his penitence by works; he had even, when in Rome, made the painful ascent of a sacred staircase on his knees to secure an indulgence for his grandfather. He had been to Rome, to the Holy City itself, and had come back unconvinced that anything he had seen demonstrated the claims of his church; indeed, he had seen much that appalled him.

The problem was that he found it impossible to turn his theological knowledge into personal peace. Whenever the priest in the confessional absolved him from his sins, Luther took them all back home with him again. Forgiveness was freely available to all, the riches of God's grace were offered to anybody who had done all that he was capable of to deserve it. But of how much, Luther wondered miserably, was Martin Luther capable? Had he really done all he could, had he left no spiritual

stone unturned? In many of his writings about those
days, he confesses that he had begun to hate God,
and to fear him: 'When I looked for Christ it seemed
to me I saw the Devil.'

As he read and re-read the Bible in preparation
for his lectures, his fascination with Paul kept him
struggling with Paul's thought, most notably the
passage in Romans:

> For in the gospel a righteousness from God is re-
> vealed, a righteousness that is by faith from first to
> last, just as it is written: 'The righteous will live by
> faith' (Rom. 1:17).

He won through to an understanding, after meditat-
ing day and night upon the passage, by considering
its context. He realised that God's grace was not a
matter of punishment but of forgiveness: that becoming acceptable to God was nothing to do with
earning salvation, but it was to do with receiving
gratefully what one could never deserve or earn.[9]

> I felt that I was altogether born again and had entered
> paradise itself through open gates. There a totally
> other face of the entire Scripture opened itself to me.
> Thereupon I ran through the Scriptures from memory.
> I also found in other terms an analogy, as, the work
> of God, that is, what God does in us, the power of
> God, with which he makes us strong, the wisdom of
> God, with which he makes us wise, the strength of
> God, the salvation of God, the glory of God. And I
> extolled my sweetest word with a love as great as the

hatred with which I had before hated the word
'righteousness of God'. Thus that place in Paul was
for me truly the gate to paradise.[10]

Kittelson quotes a moving letter of April 1516 that
illustrates the sea-change that had taken place.

Therefore ... learn Christ and him crucified; despair-
ing of yourself, learn to pray to him, saying, 'You,
Lord Jesus, are my righteousness, but I am your sin;
you have taken on yourself what you were not and
have given me what I was not.' Beware of aspiring
to such purity that you no longer wish to appear to
yourself, or to be, a sinner.[11]

PORTRAITS from those days sometimes have an
unnerving capacity to reflect real personalities;
faces like those one sees on modern streets sometimes look out of woodcuts and engravings, even
those that are crudely reproduced and primitively
drawn; all the more so with a major painter such as
Lucas Cranach, whose well-known portraits of
Luther's father and mother are so full of character
and perception that studying them helps one to
understand Luther better. Raffaelo Santi's portrait
of Pope Leo X, too, is often reproduced: the pontiff
looks oddly modern by contrast with the renaissance stereotypes who stand on either side of him.
And Cranach portrayed Martin himself more than
once, with his usual perception; the reformer's eyes
stare out at you truculently from the canvas.

So it is with a shock of recognition that one looks at contemporary engravings of Johann Tetzel, Luther's first real adversary: the overweight, dumpy figure in the pulpit, his round face and plump hands possibly betraying a well-stocked table, his eyebrows raised in a bland expression over eyes that are perhaps cold and calculating: one engraving shows large receipts piled in a box behind him ...

Yet we must be careful not to read too much into such portraits. Their artists were rarely without an axe to grind, and in any case we bring to them the hindsight of what we know today. And in the case of the travelling circus that was Tetzel's preaching crusade to Germany, we know quite a lot.

Tetzel, a Dominican friar, received in 1517 the papal commission to sell Indulgences in Germany. It was the result of an ingenious financial arrangement, part of which was to pay for the Sistine Chapel: Leo X's love of the arts had caused him severe cash-flow problems, and Indulgences were a ready means of revenue.

The principle of Indulgences was that the Church had an accumulated store of merit laid down by the saints and available for sinners, to which was added the grace of the Virgin Mary. The whole treasury was inexhaustible, because it derived from the infinite merits of Christ. Indulgences, instituted by a Bull of Pope Clement VI issued in 1343, were a means by which that grace could be used to wash away the sins of Christians now in purgatory. It was a kind of substitutionary confession, in which a living believer demonstrated his good intentions towards the church, against which demonstration could be credited the remission of sins.

It is important to remember, as Kittelson points out[12], that Indulgences were not an arbitrary concoction but a logical development of mediaeval theology; in its academic formulation, even the practice of paying money to the church was a spiritual matter, showing the sincerity of the one who paid. But even if Luther had not been struggling with a profound disagreement with his church's teaching on grace, the abuses that Tetzel represented would have been quite enough to rouse him to fury. Whatever the theologians might say, by Luther's time ordinary men and women believed that one could be freed from the penalty of sin simply by paying money. Tetzel did nothing to disabuse them, as one who saw him remarked:

> It is incredible what this ignorant and impudent friar gave out. He said that if a Christian had slept with his mother, and placed the sum of money in the Pope's indulgence chest, the Pope had power in heaven and earth to forgive the sin, and, if he forgave it, God must do so also. Item, if they contributed readily and bought grace and indulgence, all the hills of St Annaberg would become pure massive silver. Item, so soon as the coin rang in the chest, the soul for whom the money was paid would go straightway to heaven ... All the priests and monks, the town council, schoolmaster, scholars, men, women, maidens,

and children, went out to meet him with banners and tapers, with song and procession ... in short, God himself could not have been welcomed and entertained with greater honour.[13]

Luther later acknowledged the effect that the visit of 'Junker Tetzler' had on him, an effect as profound as Staupitz's teaching. He had already preached against Indulgences, but Tetzel's supermarket approach to salvation drove him to more dramatic action.

So it was that on Hallowe'en 1517, Martin Luther placed his announcement on the door of the Castle Church of Wittenberg: that he would be willing to engage in academic debate on ninety-five theses on the subject of Indulgences.

It was not an invitation to theological anarchy. It was the normal way of raising theological issues, and besides publicly announcing the agenda for his proposed disputation he also sent copies to the local church hierarchy. He wanted the church to consider its position on what was clearly a flagrant abuse. He had no intention, on 31 October 1517, of founding the Protestant church. Despite the profound spiritual change that had come over him, the Theses show a concern for the security of the church: the practice of selling Indulgences might very well bring irreparable harm to the papacy. Luther, who had no inkling of the financial deal in the Vatican that had brought Tetzel to the region, was actually warning the Pope to beware of Tetzel's activities.

The response, however, was not long in coming. Tetzel's education was rapidly completed; he was awarded his doctorate so that he could argue with Luther on equal terms. By February a new director had been appointed to the Augustinian order, commanded specifically to bring Luther to heel – this was the result of the Archbishop sending a copy of the Theses to the Pope.

Luther was pitched from obscurity to fame. Within weeks, copies of the Theses were circulating all over Germany. His university colleagues supported his cause, as did the Elector of Saxony, who had paid the fees for Luther's doctoral studies and was now highly satisfied with his protégé's illustrious academic career. But the ground was shifting in the debate: it was becoming apparent that at the heart of the issue was the question of religious authority, not least because many of those who read the Ninety-Five Theses wrongly assumed that Luther's purpose was an attack on the papacy.

He became the hero of Germany. A host of disciples joined his cause, some because they had been genuinely touched by his religious message, others because they confused their own religious or even political aspirations with his ... While some may have been strange bedfellows – mistaking Luther for a German nationalist or an Erasmian Humanist – their support was real and vastly consequential. By 1521 Luther's 'reformation' had become a popular movement. It had also become heretical.[14]

So far as Luther was concerned, his position was still that of a son of the church. He embarked on a series of lectures on the place of Indulgences in the Christian life; he continued with his other teaching; but in April he was required to explain and defend his position at a public meeting of the Augustinians at Heidelberg. But his theme there, as in all his teaching of that time, was not about the storm that had arisen over Indulgences, but about his new realisation that salvation was a gift of God's grace.

It was a far more radical suggestion than the argument against Indulgences had been, for it cut across the whole late mediaeval, scholastic view of grace. He was well received, however, and impressed some influential people. On his return he completed and published a book about the Ninety-Five Theses. In this he clarified his developing position, and for the first time explicitly criticised the theological foundation of Indulgences and the practice of confession. 'The church needs a reformation ...' he declared. 'It is the business of the entire Christian world, yes, the business of God alone.'

The book produced a response from Tetzel, whose newly-acquired doctorate added no academic distinction to a very lightweight riposte. But he did make the point that Luther had questioned the Pope's authority, which meant that Luther was a heretic. Another opponent, John Eck, expressed the same thought more elegantly: in 1519 Luther engaged in public debates with Eck at Leipzig and with Cardinal Cajetan at Augsburg. During 1520 a succession of writings from Luther's pen developed his reformational thinking, for example *The Freedom of A Christian*, based on two propositions: 'A Christian is a perfectly free lord of all and subject to no man. A Christian is a perfectly obedient servant to all and the subject of every man.'

In response, the Papal Bull *Exsurge Domine* of the same year branded Luther as a fox in the vineyard and gave him sixty days in which to recant or to present himself at Rome. He was to desist from preaching, and his books were to be burned. He should be given no shelter, and if found should be arrested.

The Elector of Saxony refused to enforce the Bull: Luther himself responded to it angrily, both in writing and in deeds: in December, he hurled a copy of the Bull into a bonfire of papal decrees and church documents. It was a public, and very festive, occasion. It was an irrevocable step: Luther explicitly accused the Pope of 'condemning the truth of God', and in the bonfire symbolically rejected the authority of the church in its decrees and its laws.

Early in 1521 the Pope issued a further, stronger Bull and ordered the Emperor to enforce it. Luther was summoned to the Diet of Worms, where in front of the Emperor he refused to recant any of his teaching unless it could be proved that the Bible contradicted him. 'Here I stand! I can do no other,' he declared. He was taken to Wartburg Castle and pronounced an outlaw; his writings were condemned.

Any hope his opponents had that he would be silenced were in vain. There was widespread support for Luther both among theologians and among the citizens of Saxony and further afield. There was now no turning back; what had begun as a theological dispute in Wittenberg had become one of the decisive historical movements of Western history.

WERE the Ninety-Five Theses the start of the Reformation?

Luther certainly did not intend them to be; the Reformation followed them only because others interpreted them as an attack on the church hierarchy and because the church hierarchy would not respond to Luther's demands for a serious reappraisal of the practice of Indulgences.

On the other hand, Luther in 1517 was set on a course that would inevitably have brought confrontation sooner or later. His theological development, his dissatisfaction with the mediatorial role of the clergy, his fury at abuses that deceived ordinary people and dishonoured Christ and his clergy, would all have led to a stand sooner or later. It is perhaps appropriate – and characteristic of the irenical professor of Wittenberg – that Luther only took to campaigning, preaching and writing against Rome when attempts to persuade the Pope to conform to biblical teaching failed.

Because that was the sequence of events, the charge that the Reformation was a reaction to local and contemporary abuses, a movement that has lost relevance in later centuries, cannot be laid at Luther's door. It was the theology that Luther finally broke with, not its distortions. It was not the embarrassing posturing of Tetzel that moved him, but his growing mistrust of the whole practice of ecclesiastical absolution. And that had been growing long before Tetzel arrived in Saxony, as Luther's earlier writings show.

Notes

1. H. A. L. Fisher, *A History of Europe* (Arnold, 1936), p.500.
2. Owen Chadwick, *The Reformation* (Penguin, rev edn 1972), p.51.
3. James Atkinson, *Martin Luther and the Birth of Protestantism* (Penguin, 1968), p.11.
4. James M. Kittelson, *Luther the Reformer* (1986: IVP, 1989), p.299.
5. Quoted by L. W. Cowie, *The Reformation of the Sixteenth Century* (Wayland, 1970), pp. 17-18.
6. L. W. Cowie, *Luther* (Weidenfeld & Nicolson, 1968), p.115.
7. 'Preface to the First Volume of Latin Writings' (1545): in *Works*, vol. 34, ed L. W. Spitz (Philadelphia, 1960), pp.336-7.
8. Quoted by V. H. H. Green, *Luther and the Reformation* (1964: Batsford, 1974), p.50.
9. Luther's theological development is long and complex: only the bare bones of it can be sketched here. In particular the exact date of Luther's final realisation of salvation by faith – his 'tower

experience' – is uncertain. Kittelson and Atkinson (both *op. cit.*)
both devote considerable space to Luther's spiritual search.

10. 'Preface to the First Volume of the Latin Writings', pp.336-7.

11. James M. Kittelson, *op. cit.*, p.95.

12. James M. Kittelson, *ibid.*, pp.101ff.

13. B. J. Kidd, *Documents Illustrative of the Continental Reformation* (OUP, 1911), p.19, quoted in L. W. Cowie, *op. cit.*

14. Hans J. Hillebrand, ed., *The Protestant Reformation: Selected Documents* (MacMillan, 1968), p.xv.

3

John Bunyan
Arrest and Imprisonment

There are some legends of the Christian church that we are reluctant to lose, even when they prove unfounded. Perhaps one of those that survives most tenaciously is that there was once an uneducated tinker, John Bunyan, who, it is said, wrote an imperishable book while incarcerated in a lonely prison, and never failed to produce enduring literature whenever he picked up his pen.

As is so often the case, the legend tends to disparage the extraordinary work of God in the life of John Bunyan. To regard all his many books as masterpieces diminishes the brilliance of the handful of titles that made Bunyan immortal. To interpret his imprisonment (which allowed him the opportunity to read and to preach to the other dissenters who shared his crowded prison) as a lonely martyrdom hardly helps us to understand the heroism of his life as a whole. To consider Bunyan as an illiterate who managed to produce a masterpiece is to ignore the weight of learning contained in his prolific writings. And to see him as a solitary beacon in a Godless age ignores the complex cross-currents of thought in seventeenth-century England – just as the Wesleyan revival of the next century is sometimes wrongly regarded as a fire of true faith in an England dominated by a moribund Anglican Church; 'true faith' is accurate, but 'moribund' would be a severe over-simplification. Even to take Bunyan's own testimony of his own extreme pre-conversion sinfulness is to misunderstand the literary form in which *Grace Abounding to the Chief of Sinners* is written, and what Bunyan expected his testimony to achieve for his fellow church-members and also what they expected writing it would achieve for him.

The mistake that many who have wanted to honour John Bunyan have made is to see him as a genuine original, sprung fully-formed on to the stage of history. But he was a man shaped by the complex world in which he lived and the patterns of religious and secular thought that influenced it. Which by no means diminishes the fact that his most significant book, *The Pilgrim's Progress*, is an incomparable masterpiece; nor that for centuries it was one of the handful of books that could be found in almost every literate English-speaking home.

WE possess an unusually full transcript of the trial of John Bunyan at Bedford on the January 1661 Quarter Sessions. It was written by Bunyan himself.[1] He had been a recognised preacher since 1657, and the discriminatory legislation passed after the Restoration of 1660 had brought him before the court. Bunyan's transcript has the ring of truth, chiefly in its lack of any attempt to present its author in a particularly clever, learned or spiritual light; the factually presented dialogue is almost relaxed at times. It was not unusual for independent nonconformists like Bunyan to record such transcripts; they served as reminders that they too had been tried before magistrates just as the apostles had, and it is unlikely that Bunyan would, even from worthy motives, have written down substantially different to what was actually said.

He had come a long way since his birth at Elstow in 1628, the son of a yeoman tinker, a trade which he followed after his brief education until enlisting in the Parliamentary side in 1644 in the Civil War. His family was not so obscure and impoverished as Bunyan suggests in his writings; there had been Bunyans in that part of Bedfordshire for 300 years, and the name appears frequently in transactions of land. Though down on their luck by the time John was born, the Bunyans were by no means paupers. Their cottage stood in nine acres of land.

His education was scanty, but he learned to read and write. It is not known for sure whether he learned much more – whether, for example, he was taught Latin or read any of the classical authors. His own description of his education tells us little.

> Notwithstanding the meanness and inconsiderable-
> ness of my Parents, it pleased God to put it into their
> heart, to put me to School, to learn both to Read and
> Write; the which I also attained, according to the rate
> of other poor mens children, though to my shame I
> confess, I did soon loose that little I learned, even
> almost utterly, and that long before the Lord did
> work his gracious work of conversion upon my
> Soul.[2]

However, though he lacked formal education, his
work bears the fruit of systematic study not only of
the Bible but of other books as well; for example,
his earliest stirrings of religious concern were fed
by two popular religious handbooks:

> [My first wife] had for her part, *The Plain Mans
> Path-Way to Heaven*, and *The Practice of Piety*,
> which her Father had left her when he died. In these
> two books I should sometimes read with her, where-
> in I found some things that were somewhat pleasing
> to me.[3]

His own writing does not follow contemporary
literary fashion, but neither is his lean, brilliantly-
observed narrative simply the spontaneous conversation of an uneducated man. Those who analyse
Bunyan's writing analyse it as literature, not as
naive, primitive folk art. Thus for example his
biographer, John Brown, contributed one of the
first discussions of Bunyan's literary merits, albeit
in a book on preaching.[4]

Preaching was far from the young John Bunyan's mind when he left school to follow his father's trade; he may well have also helped tend his father's acres. In *Grace Abounding to the Chief of Sinners* he portrays himself as a carefree youth, playing games on the village green and living a thoroughly secular life. Yet there was also already evidence of a troubled spirit, of occasional dreams and forebodings that filled him with dread. When he was sixteen his mother died, followed a month later by his sister. The month after that, his father married for the third time, a situation that did little to bring him peace of mind.

They were troubled times in which he lived. Puritanism, which had begun in 1560 as an appeal for a 'more Godly thorough Reformation' of the English church, was in the ascendant during his early years.

The influence of Puritanism ran underground while Charles I and Archbishop Laud governed England, but that did not stop the influence being powerful. The force that created New England could not be impotent in the colonists' home country.[5]

By the mid-seventeenth century the ecclesiastical protest had become a political cause ready to go to war, and the English monarchy had only a few short years left before the execution of Charles I in 1649 – when Bunyan was just twenty-one years old – and the proclamation of the Commonwealth.

The Civil War began in 1642. In 1644 Bunyan joined the Parliamentary Army, but though he remained a soldier until 1647 he saw no action in the English Civil War. It was in the Army, however, that although 'the thought of religion was very grievous' to him he came under the influence of the radical Puritan 'preaching captains'. He was challenged by the enthusiasm of these unorthodox and uncontrollable preachers, who were at their most active during the years of his army service. As Cromwell observed to Parliament in 1657,

> I must say to you on behalf of our Army – in the next place to their fighting they have been very good preachers ... they have been accustomed to preach to their troops, companies and regiments – which I think has been one of the blessings upon them to the carrying on of the great work.[6]

From the army preachers Bunyan heard of a religion that taught salvation wholly by faith, and of a faith that intended to change the world. It was in the army, too, that he experienced the daily routines of barracks life that were to find their way into print in some of the most attractive passages of *The Holy War*.

Bunyan was demobilised in 1647. Shortly afterwards he married and set up home in Elstow; his wife owned the two devotional books mentioned earlier, and these joined the Bible, the Prayer Book and Foxe's *Book of Martyrs* as Bunyan's reading

matter. It was the beginning of a time of spiritual
self-searching and torment that is recorded in detail
in *Grace Abounding*. His wife, about whom next to
nothing is known, came from a godly home; Bunyan makes a point of recording his father-in-law's
piety and personal integrity. Of the two books that
he says they studied together, Arthur Dent's *Plain
Mans Path-Way to Heaven* certainly influenced his
own writing, especially *Pilgrim's Progress*.

He abandoned his worldly pleasures and enter-
tainments in his quest for personal faith, and painstakingly tackled the externals of religious duty,
influenced by the army preachers' sermons, the
example of his wife, and a deep unsettling conviction that he was a sinner who needed to be reconciled to God. In response to the prevailing mood of
the age he gave up his hobby of bell-ringing, and
tried hard to stop swearing, a habit to which he had
been addicted. He attended church, paying great
respect to outward ceremonial and vestments, and
became obsessed with obscure theological conun-
drums.

One Sunday, he was stricken with remorse when
the vicar preached against Sunday entertainment.
Somehow he managed to shake off the oppressive
conviction of sin this produced in him; the mood
passed: 'the fire was put out, that I might sin again
without control!'.

LATER that same Sunday he was playing tip-cat, an ancient game played with a wooden bat and 'cat' or puck:

> Just as I was about to strike it the second time, a voice did suddenly dart from heaven into my Soul, which said, *Wilt thou leave thy sins, and go to Heaven? or have thy sins, and go to Hell?* At this I was put to an exceeding maze; wherefore, leaving my Cat upon the ground, I looked up to Heaven, and was as if I had with the eyes of my understanding, seen the Lord Jesus looking down upon me, as being very hotly displeased with me, and as if he did severely threaten me with some grievous punishment for these, and my other ungodly practices.[7]

It is an indication of Bunyan's gifts as a writer that *Grace Abounding* takes its place as one of the most profound psychological studies of conversion ever written. He records a miserable repentance, groaning under the burden of God's wrath, striving to live according to God's law and bitterly aware of his failings – failings which his neighbours were only too ready to point out to him in case he had not noticed them himself. Like Luther and many more before and since, he was a man being slowly and surely killed by law and searching in vain for grace.

In Bedford one day he overheard 'three or four poor women sitting at a door in the Sun, and talking about the things of God'. He was shaken, for he recognised that these women had experienced something of which he, in all his spiritual quests, had remained utterly ignorant: the 'new birth, the work of God on their hearts'. He found himself making opportunities to pass that way again, and to visit them often. Soon he was being pulled two ways: by the godly teaching of the Bedford women who spoke of undeserved grace and a new birth, and his own conviction that salvation demanded from him a huge effort of the will and a laborious fulfilling of the law's demands.

'What would the devil do for company were it not for such as me?' joked a former friend, a prolific swearer just as Bunyan had been; but Bunyan was appalled at his frivolity. He looked into the teaching of the Ranters, who argued that they were exempt from the law, and was similarly appalled. When others accused him, with some justice, of being obsessed with legalism, he saw it as an attempt to sway him from the path of repentance.

It was, he recognised in *Grace Abounding*, God alone who preserved him from such temptations, and put into his heart a longing for God and a fascination with the Bible, which now became to him like a new and absorbing book:

Especially the Epistles of the Apostle St Paul were sweet and pleasant to me: and indeed, I was never out of the Bible, either by reading or meditation, still crying out to God, that I might know the truth, and the way to Heaven and Glory.[8]

He read 1 Corinthians 12:8ff and wondered whether he had any faith at all, and how to tell if he had. He thought he would test his faith by trying to work a miracle, and commanded the puddles on the Bedford road to dry up. When they did not, he suspected that this only confirmed his plight.

As he struggled 'betwixt the devil and my own ignorance', he had a vision. He saw the poor people of Bedford on the sunlit slopes of a high mountain, basking in the sun, and he himself shivering in snow. Between them stood a wall that encircled the mountain and which he longed to cross. After much searching he found a tiny gap through which, with great struggles, he managed to pass and so was able to join the believers and share in the warmth of the sun.

It was not a difficult vision to interpret. Bunyan readily grasped its meaning: the mountain was the church; the wall, the world; the gate, Jesus Christ, through whom was access, but only for those who were in great earnest. It was the beginning of a slow path to salvation. The Bedford Christians told their pastor, John Gifford, about the distressed young man who was in such spiritual anguish, and Gifford befriended him.

The Independent congregation that Bunyan had encountered in Bedford was a newly-established one. Gifford was a colourful character who had been a major on the King's side in the Civil War and had escaped from a condemned cell to hide in

Bedford. Then he became a doctor, a Christian and a Puritan, and when the Bedford Puritans decided to establish a church or 'meeting' in 1650 they invited Gifford – who was a gifted preacher – to be their leader.

'Bunyan Meeting', as it became known later, was forward-looking in many ways, and on matters such as baptism Gifford, a Baptist by conviction, was tolerant of other views, as was his successor John Burton. Gifford took a liking to Bunyan and invited him to his home, where he heard others talk about 'the dealings of God with the Soul'. Gradually, under the ministry of Gifford and his flock, Bunyan's struggles became permeated with an awareness of God's love, unmerited and undeserved. 'Oh!' he records, 'now, how was my Soul led from truth to truth by God! even from the birth and cradle of the Son of God, to his ascension and second coming from Heaven to judge the World.'

> Truly, I then found upon this account the great God was very Good unto me, for to my remembrance there was not any thing that I then cried unto God to make known and reveal unto me but he was pleased to do it for me, I mean not one part of the Gospel of the Lord Jesus, but I was orderly led into it ...[9]

The end of his spiritual quest saw him in 1653 received into Gifford's congregation. It is probable that his account of his path to conversion, which like all new members he was required to give to the

Meeting, formed the basis of the later *Grace Abounding to the Chief of Sinners*. His gifts were quickly recognised and he acquired a growing reputation for his sermons which were at first delivered to private gatherings. When Gifford died in 1655 to be succeeded in the pastorate by the frail John Burton, Bunyan began to be called upon to preach in public and in 1657 was given formal recognition as a preacher.

More than sixty of Bunyan's writings survive, and many of them are little more than transcripts of sermons. It is possible to see from them the energy of his preaching, and to sense a little of the impact that he had on his hearers; and to see too Bunyan's qualities as a debater and controversialist – in which he practised well the rough, often savage rhetoric of his time. Traces of the debates in which he was involved can be found in the speeches given to some of his best-known characters, and in the names that some of them bear.

As an out-of-town member (he still lived at Elstow) he was active in pastoral care, travelling widely on church business; had he remained in one place and worked either as a tinker or a preacher, the world might have been deprived of many of the characters of his great works, for they have the unmistakable look of portraits drawn from life, noted no doubt for future use as Bunyan travelled the roads, towns and villages of the county.

He was a father now. He had two daughters, one

of whom was born blind. His wife was to bear him two more children before her death in 1658, three years after the family moved to Bedford to be more fully involved in the Meeting. She had played a major part in her husband's progress to faith, and Bunyan willingly acknowledges that fact in *Grace Abounding*. Nobody who reads that book can doubt either her influence or Bunyan's gratitude. It is with something of a shock that one realises that we do not even know her name.

She lived to see her husband launched as an author: Bunyan's first book, *Some Gospel Truths Opened*, appeared in 1656. It was an attack on Quaker beliefs, for Bunyan was alarmed at the growing influence of the new movement, founded in 1648 by George Fox, which had Baptist roots and taught doctrines which he deplored. Bunyan was prompted to write because of public debates in Bedford in which Edward Burroughs the Quaker was involved. Burroughs took up Bunyan's arguments, provoking a second tract by Bunyan.

He remarried in 1659: his wife Elizabeth was later to report to him the words she spoke in his defence at his trial, from which she emerges as a spirited and persuasive woman:

My Lord, said she, I was a-while since at London, to see if I could get my husband's liberty, and there I spoke with my Lord Bedford, one of the house of

Lords, to whom I delivered a petition, who took it of
me and presented it to some of the rest of the house
of Lords, for my husband's releasement ... they said,
that they could not release him, but had committed
his releasement to the Judges, at the next assises.
This he told me; and now I come to you to see if any
thing may be done in this business, and you give
neither releasement nor relief ...[10]

One year after Bunyan's second marriage, Charles
II ascended the throne and the monarchy was restored. Puritan ministers in the Church of England
who persisted in rejecting the Prayer Book were
ejected from their posts. The Puritans, from being
the rulers, became a minority nonconformist church
that attracted unwelcome attention from the newly
re-established authorities. John Burton the pastor
of the Bedford Meeting died in 1660, several months
after the Restoration. The loss soon became a
double one, for in November of that year Bunyan
found himself brought before the local magistrate.

He was not arrested under the new Restoration
measures, but under an Elizabethan Act against
nonconformists. A warrant was issued to arrest him
while preaching at Samsell, near Bedford. Word of
the planned arrest came to Bunyan secretly before-
hand, but he declined to 'play the coward', even
though he was under the impression that his life was
at risk.

For his refusal to stop preaching, Bunyan was
detained in the Bedford county gaol, to appear at

the Quarter Sessions the following January. The trial (which is meticulously reported in *A Relation of the Imprisonment of Mr John Bunyan*) was before a judge, Sir John Keeling, who was a rapidly rising star in the new establishment. Bunyan's account is a valuable document.

> To hear a man like Keeling exchanging scripture arguments with the nonconformist tinker is to be taken inside the seventeenth-century mind. 'It is lawful to use Common Prayer and such like forms: for Christ taught his disciples to pray, as John also taught his disciples ... Faith comes by hearing.' Later when Keeling begins to bluster, Bunyan stands unmoved, abiding by his texts with a pedantic but sublime literalness.[11]

Bunyan's refusal to stop preaching was an extremely brave decision. The penalty for repeated offences was further prison sentences and eventually transportation. If he had chosen, he could have limited his preaching to private groups in domestic homes, and the authorities would not have pursued him. Instead he went to prison, being specifically excluded from the amnesty that was announced for the Coronation in April. His wife, who had a miscarriage when her husband was arrested, appealed at the Midsummer Assizes unsuccessfully, and later appeals for clemency and parole were turned down.

In the County Jail in Bedford Bunyan made

bootlaces to support his family, preached to other
prisoners, received a flow of visitors and was even
allowed out occasionally – in the early days, before
the 1662 enactments became a strict control on
dissenters, and at the end of his imprisonment after
1668 when he was allowed some parole. But what
marks his imprisonment as a key stage in his life is
that in prison he began to write his major works.
Grace Abounding to the Chief of Sinners appeared
in 1666: Bunyan's powerful awareness of his own
path to conversion and of God's hand in his life
invested what was a well-known form of Reformed
church testimony with a rare psychological profun-
dity. He wrote a number of other works during this
period, of varying quality, including some verse:
while he was not a gifted poet, he has a place in the
history of children's literature for his didactic em-
blematic stanzas.

Released in 1672 (partly at the request of his old
adversaries the Quakers, for the pardon that accompanied Charles II's Declaration of Indulgence that
year largely benefited them), Bunyan resumed his
work, having been elected pastor of the church
while still in prison. The new atmosphere of toler-
ance permitted him to obtain a licence to preach
publicly, though religious freedom was by no means
fully restored; and his 'parish' included a number
of churches in the surrounding area that were associated with the Bedford Meeting. He also preached
in London, and there are indications that he enjoyed

a very distinguished contemporary reputation as a preacher; it is said that he travelled as far afield as Leicester and Cambridgeshire. Certainly, like John Wesley after him, he spent a great deal of time reading on horseback.

He was also an articulate and forceful controversialist, for example in his pamphlet war with the Anglican Edward Fowler over justification by faith. Bunyan had clearly read Fowler's writings in prison, and launched an angry and aggressive response (Fowler responded likewise under the title *Dirt Wip'd Off*).

The Declaration of Indulgence was a short-lived respite. It was repealed, and persecution of dissenters returned: in 1675 a warrant was issued against him, clearly instigated by his old opponents. In 1677 Bunyan found himself in prison again. During his six-month sentence he completed *Pilgrim's Progress,* which he must have been contemplating during his first imprisonment and which he stocked with characters and ideas drawn from life. His release was in part due to the efforts of his admirer John Owen, leader of the Independents, one of the great theologians of the time, and former chaplain to Oliver Cromwell.[12] In 1678 *Pilgrim's Progress* was published, and Bunyan became a celebrity; even his printer became famous.

In 1680 *The Life and Death of Mr Badman* appeared. While it cannot be compared with his great masterpiece, the book does provide much

valuable material for social historians and makes
its theological points competently if somewhat
glumly. *The Holy War*, published in 1682, was a
more appropriate book for an author who by now
was celebrated. Its central image is a stirring one,
its characters are intriguing, and though none have
the rich roundedness of most of the characters of
Pilgrim's Progress, the book lives and breathes the
authentic air of the late seventeenth century. The
cosmic struggle for the soul of humanity reaches
some genuinely tragic heights in Bunyan's hands.

Bunyan's fame increased, though he was never
entirely free from the fear that he might be arrested
yet again. He was still writing: many of the books
and pamphlets of this period are sermon notes
barely reshaped into book form, and while they are
of interest to few today except those interested in
the period's controversies and theological cross-
currents, they do indicate the punishing schedule
Bunyan was setting himself.

His last major book was Part II of *Pilgrim's
Progress*, written in part to satisfy the demand for
a sequel (and out of annoyance because others had
tried to do so), but also because Bunyan proposes a
quite different tale: that of the Christian family, the
church, reflected in the account of Christian's wife
Christiana who follows her husband on his path to
salvation. Sometimes neglected even by people
who enjoyed Part I, it has its own great passages
(such as the death of Mr Valiant-for-Truth), and

some surprises for those who think that life in a Puritan home must have been a tedious and strictly humourless affair: minstrels entertain at the Interpreter's House, at Gaius's inn the family is entertained with riddles, and Mr Greatheart provides wine and good food for the journey and contributes an elaborate parable based on musical theory. Indeed, the book is full of music, good food and fellowship.

At the end of his life he was once again harassed for his beliefs, and finally benefited from James II's policy of toleration towards dissenters, intended to pave the way for toleration towards Roman Catholics. It is typical of the ironies of the time that Bunyan should more than once have owed his freedom to those with whom he was locked in theological controversy.

He seems to have had considerable pastoral gifts, and it is characteristic of him that his death in 1688 came about as a result of a fever which he had contracted while riding to preach: he had taken the opportunity to halt his journey and reconcile two brothers who had been quarrelling. He completed his journey in pouring rain and died soon afterwards.

Bunyan is buried in Bunhill Fields, near William Blake and Daniel Defoe: an old plague-pit, it was, between 1695 and 1852, the principal burying place of nonconformists in London. In Bunhill Row nearby, that other great English Christian writer, John Milton, completed his epic *Paradise Lost*.

THE legacy of Bunyan is a moving one. He had a simple certainty in the correctness of his own beliefs, and was not swayed when influential and powerful people attempted to force him to abandon them. His pastoral and preaching ministries were powerful, and there is evidence in his later life that had he not chosen to throw in his lot with the Bedford congregation but had moved to London or looked for a more strategic pastorate, he might have become as great a figure as John Owen. The fact that he stayed where he was and remained a journeyman tinker for most of his life, gave him access to the ordinary everyday people and sights of English common life that adorn his books. The fact that he went to prison rather than abandon his call to preach undoubtedly gave him time to conceive and complete his major works. It may well be that absence from the sophisticated church circles of London helped him retain that unerring ear for English common speech that gives his prose its sinewy vigour.

But it is the Puritan dynamic that marks his work, far more than the authentic Bedfordshire scene-setting. What leaps from the page across the centuries is Bunyan's vision of a world in which one leaves the known and loved and trusted, in search of the Celestial City, along a road that is straddled by giants and near which mountains burst into flames; a world in which armies wheel and clash in their attempts to take the castle of the soul, where the death of a Badman is so peaceful that the reader is repulsed, where once one has understood the spiritual landscape of Bunyan's world, a game of tip-cat on the village green can fill one with dread because one sees how near the pit the worldly young man is straying.

It was a transforming force in English literature, in a century in which Puritanism touched and changed most things. When the energy of the Puritan revolution subsided and the monarchy reasserted itself, the dynamic of the God who might at any moment intervene in his own creation continued to fire the Christian mind. It was a dynamic that was vital groundwork for the Evangelical revival of the following century; it foreshadowed the Romantic movement, and its roots touched the European ideas that were to culminate in the French Revolution. Bunyan lived his life in the shadow of a political revolution, but his writing and his faith expound a spiritual revolution of much greater significance.

Notes

1. John Bunyan, *A Relation of the Imprisonment of Mr. John Bunyan* (first published 1765).
2. John Bunyan, *Grace Abounding to the Chief of Sinners* (ed. John Sharrock, OUP, 1966), p.7.
3. *Ibid*, p.10.
4. John Brown, 'John Bunyan as a Life-Study for Preachers': in *Puritan Preaching in England: a Study Past and Present* (1900), pp.131-164.
5. David L. Edwards, *Christian England* (Collins, rev. edn 1989), ii.255.
6. Quoted in C. H. Firth, *Cromwell's Army* (Methuen, 3rd edn 1921), p.336.
7. *Grace Abounding*, p.12.
8. *Ibid*, p.19.
9. *Ibid*, p.39.
10. John Bunyan, *A Relation of the Imprisonment of Mr. John Bunyan* (ed. John Sharrock, OUP, 1966), p.131.
11. Roger Sharrock, *John Bunyan* (MacMillan, 1954), p.40.
12. F. M. Harrison quotes Owen as saying to Charles II that he would 'willingly exchange all his learning for the tinker's power of touching men's hearts.' (*John Bunyan*, 1928: Banner of Truth, edn 1964), p.159.

4

The Conversion of John Wesley

At five o'clock on the morning of Wednesday, 24 May 1738, in a lodging house not far from St Paul's Cathedral in London, a man in his mid-thirties reached for his Greek New Testament and began to read. As was his custom, he let the book fall open at random. Much later he wrote in his journal the verses that he read that morning: 'There are given unto us exceeding great and precious promises, even that ye should be partakers of the divine nature', and 'Thou art not far from the kingdom of God.'[1]

It was the beginning of a day which was to become famous throughout the world: writing about it, the historian John Lecky would describe it as 'an epoch in English history'. The man was John Wesley, a striking-looking figure of medium height, the severity of his features emphasised by an angular nose and large eyes but softened by a surprisingly gentle, even humorous mouth and unfashionably long and glossy hair. The clothes in which Wesley dressed himself that morning were sober ecclesiastical garb, the attire of a minister in the Church of England and appropriate for a missionary newly returned from the New Colonies. The day was the day of his conversion.

Clerical black suited Wesley's mood, for since his return from America he had been profoundly ill-at-ease.

The son of an Anglican rector, Samuel Wesley, and his remarkable wife Susanna who bore Samuel nineteen children and ruled her family with love, learning and considerable spiritual strength, John Wesley had entered Oxford in 1720. He had been appalled at the ungodly life led by students and staff, and determined to live in an exemplary fashion and enter the Anglican priesthood. Four years later he took his degree and in 1725, with his parents' blessing, was ordained as a deacon in the Church of England. The following year he was elected a Fellow of Lincoln College Oxford, which secured him accommodation and income while he remained unmarried.

There had always been an ascetic streak in Wesley. At the age of five he had been snatched from a blaze at the family home, Epworth Rectory in Lincolnshire. The sense of divine protection that had marked his escape – 'a brand plucked from the burning' – never left him. As a boy of eleven at the Charterhouse School he had read his Bible, said his prayers, and striven mightily to do good works; he reflected in later life,

> What I now hoped to be saved by was, (1) not being so bad as other people; (2) having still a kindness for religion; and (3) reading the Bible, going to Church, and saying my prayers.

As an Oxford undergraduate he disapproved of the moral laxity of student life but struggled with his own liking for light fiction and plays. Though Oxford was in decline during the period, his tutors were learned and able teachers, and Wesley embarked upon a brilliant academic career: had he never become a preacher, his work in education and his writings would have secured him a permanent place in eighteenth-century English history. He set himself the discipline of maintaining a spiritual diary – a habit which Charles, who arrived in Oxford as a student in 1726 and was prone to worldly 'diversions', also adopted. But Charles did not share John's enthusiasm for godly living, though he was already displaying the gift for writing verse which was to make him England's greatest hymn writer. At that time, however, he saw piety as something that could safely be left for later and spent his first year in Oxford having as enjoyable a time as possible.

John spent the next two years on leave of absence from the College, working as his elderly father's curate. He enjoyed sport and dancing, and taught himself to play the flute; and there was a visit to a London theatre with Charles which left Charles briefly infatuated with an actress and John tortured by doubts about whether theatre was a legitimate entertainment for Christians. After the visit John travelled with his brother back to Oxford, where Charles was to resume his studies and John was to receive his final ordination from the Bishop of Oxford. Whether it was because he realised that his flirtation with the actress was getting him into very deep waters, or because of John's efforts during the journey to persuade him of his folly, Charles returned to the university sobered by his adventure. He embarked on a new regime of Christian reading and prayer, and was soon as well-known as a religious young man as he had been as an under-graduate-about-town.

John himself finally returned to his college in 1729 and soon became the leader of a small group which Charles had formed with other like-minded students. When some months later the group began to engage in social work, they formed themselves into a society with strict rules, a mutual commitment to spiritual self-scrutiny, and an austere life-style. The group's welfare activities, at least, were in a long tradition of university charity; but the group was ridiculed by students and dons and quickly acquired the nickname 'Holy Club'. The emphasis on religious duty and discipline earned them the further label of 'methodists'.

The members of the Holy Club tried all the more determinedly to lead exemplary and spiritual lives. Introduced by a friend to the practice of fasting, they began to do so twice a week; the Wesleys' parents, at first glad to see their sons wanting to help the poor, were less impressed when they refused to eat with the family on a visit home. Susanna Wes-

ley afterwards wrote them a characteristically sting-
ing letter. It was useless. John and Charles were
bent on good works. If the rising tide of antagonism
in Oxford against the 'methodists' had not put them
off, parental protests were even less likely to do so.

In 1735 Samuel Wesley died. Attempts to gain
the Rectorship of Epworth for John were unsuccessful, and the family home broke up: the Wesleys
were scattered. John stayed on as acting rector for
two months, then went on to London where a
chance meeting resulted in both John and Charles
deciding to go as missionaries to Georgia, an American colony in the Indian Savannah: its founder was
looking for new clergy and invited the Holy Club –
now numbering fourteen members – to go there.

The scheme offered ample scope for deepening
and extending the asceticism that the group had
practised in Oxford. It provided a supreme opportunity for service, for good deeds. It was, as friends
pointed out, a chance to do practically what had
been advocated intellectually for several years. The
Indians were heathens, in need of the gospel, with
souls destined for a godless eternity. One particular
attraction for John was that it lessened the probabil-
ity of being tempted by women (he considered that
Indian women were not likely to be physically
desirable), and as the stipend was small, asceticism
and simple living would be easy to achieve.

Charles was hurriedly ordained and on 14 October 1735 the brothers set sail for Georgia. In the

event only four members of the Holy Club went to
Georgia, the other two being Benjamin Ingham and
Charles Delamotte. During the voyage they adopted a strict regime of prayer, Bible reading, fasting,
study and worship. For the latter they sometimes
joined with a group of twenty-six Germans emi-
grating to America because of religious persecution at home; they were members of the Moravian
Church, humble, radiant people who sang psalms
and hymns with a warmth that made the Holy
Club's Anglican chants seem chilly by comparison. The Moravians, intrigued and somewhat dis-
mayed by the austerity of the four Englishmen,
asked them some searching questions. By the time
the ship reached Georgia, Wesley was aware that
there was a huge difference between his own dogged
attempts to satisfy God's demands and the Moravian
teaching of justification by faith alone. When John
asked them for some guidance on his new job, he
encountered an unexpected cross-examination by
their leader, Spangenberg.

'Do you know Jesus Christ?'

'I know he is the Saviour of the world.' Wesley's
response was theologically flawless, but
Spangenberg would not let him escape.

'True, but do you know he has died to save you?'

'I hope he has died to save me,' declared Wesley.

'Do you *know*, yourself?' pressed the other.

'I do,' replied Wesley automatically, but confessed later to his journal, 'I fear they were vain words.'

The Moravians impressed Wesley most by their behaviour when the ship encountered a raging storm. During a worship service, when the Moravians were singing a psalm, the sea broke over the ship and poured on to the decks. The Moravians calmly sang on. After the storm abated, Wesley sought out one of the Germans. 'Were you not afraid?' he asked. The German shook his head. 'I thank God, no ... Our women and children are not afraid to die.'

Characteristically, Wesley immediately used the incident as sermon material to exhort other less tranquil passengers. But he knew that it was a sermon he needed to preach to himself. He was aware of a lack of peace, of an absence of assurance of salvation. Asked before embarking what his purpose was in going to Georgia, he had said: 'To preach the gospel to the Indians, and to save my own soul.' By the time he reached America, the salvation of his soul had become a priority.

AND now it was two-and-a-half years later and Wesley was back in London.

The time in Georgia had been disastrous, by his own admission. Charles, whose official post was Secretary to the governor Colonel Oglethorpe, was ineffective at his job and never mastered it; eventually, worn out by arguments with his employer, burdened by a sense of failure in evangelising the Indians, and in poor health, he returned to England, leaving his brother in Georgia. By then, the initial good impression John's congregation had gained of their hard-working and dedicated new clergy-man had been dissipated by irritation at his old-fashioned view of liturgy and the introduction of fasting and other practices learned from his Oxford days – practices not only irksome but suspiciously similar to 'popish' rituals. Inexperience, an inflex-ible attitude to church services and some often insensitive choices of sermon text might all have been overcome in time. But – ironically, as he had expected women to be the least of his worries in Georgia – it was a woman, Sophy Hopkey, who brought the young missionary's career to an end.

The clumsy courtship, the accusations and coun-ter-accusations of broken promises and misleading commitments, and Wesley's subsequent public blundering in excommunicating Sophy all involved no sexual immorality. But the episode left him miserably aware that his own motives in the rela-tionship had been neither fair to Sophy nor spiritu-ally pure: 'I find I cannot take fire into my bosom and not be burnt.' The excommunication, on an ecclesiastical technicality, had all the signs of sour grapes. When the matter flared into a public trial for defamation and a major split over the matter in the Georgia community, Wesley decided to abandon his defence and go back to England. To do so he had to leave secretly; he was breaking his bail and also his contract of employment.

'I went to America to convert the Indians,' he wrote. 'But oh, who will convert me?' He was aware of the collapse of his missionary hopes. He had seen the scandal that had surrounded his unhappy courtship. He was shaken by the public contempt in which many of his flock now held him, and he knew all too well the disappointment of those who had seen him embark for Georgia. But he had more profound disquiet too. He had discovered, in his short career abroad, that he had been simply 'beating the air'; dangers at sea had reminded him that he was not ready to face death, and his years of diligent religious observance had proved to be a poor substitute for the happy spirituality of the Moravians who cared little for fasts and praying-by-the-hour. In numerous writings then and later, published and private, Wesley revealed that he was grappling with the biggest question of all: was he – after a Christian upbringing, ordination, religious observance and missionary service – even a Christian?

There were some positive aspects; the experience had not been a total failure. Wesley returned to England on 1 February to discover that another Oxford friend, George Whitefield, had on that very tide set out for Georgia. Like several members of the original Holy Club, Whitefield had moved

away from the legalism of the small Oxford group.
His preaching had already sparked a revival in
Bristol and his last sermons before leaving for
Georgia had been preached to emotional crowds.
His message – that grace was free and did not have
to be earned – could hardly have been more different to Wesley's. But his personal respect and affection for the older man was unchanged. Now he had
followed him to America. Wesley contemplated
meeting with Whitefield, whose ship was still lying
off the coast, to warn him about events in the
colony: but after considering the difficulty of reaching the ship he decided not to attempt it. On arrival
Whitefield refused to express an opinion about the
dispute and wrote generously about Wesley's work
in Georgia. It is unlikely that he would have fabri-
cated evidence for his predecessor's enduring results, and so it would seem that Wesley's ministry
in Savannah was – to some extent at least – more
fruitful than he believed, though it is probable too
that Whitefield took care to present what fruit there
was in the best possible light:

> The good [that] Mr Wesley has done, under God, in
> America is inexpressible. His name is very precious
> among the people; and he has laid such a foundation,
> that I hope neither men nor devils will ever be able to
> shake. Oh, that I may follow him, as he has Christ!

Common sense and an examination of Wesley's
own journal indicates that Whitefield was probably

placing on record – for the sake of the Wesleys' rehabilitation in England and the forwarding of the work of the Georgia mission – the rather limited number of people who had responded favourably to Wesley's personal integrity, hard work for the gospel, and emphasis on Christian duty and traditionalist worship forms.

It was, too, a time of training and consolidation, as all first appointments tend to be in any walk of life. In Georgia Wesley continued his studies and had the opportunity to test some of his theories, with variable results. But he was also able to continue his contacts with the Moravians; his awareness of his own spiritual need grew alarmingly.

> Being ignorant of the righteousness of Christ, which, by a living faith in him, bringeth salvation 'to every one that believeth' I sought to establish my own righteousness, and so laboured in the fire all my days.

The more he saw of the Moravians, the more he knew his need of salvation; and if it took failure, scandal and a law-suit to drive the point home, the experience cannot be said to have been entirely unprofitable.

HE described his spiritual condition on his return to England as ignorance of his complete lack of faith: he 'only thought that I had not enough of it'. Determined to embark once more on an even more

rigorous pursuit of personal piety, he was non-
plussed when six days after his return he met Peter
Bohler, a Moravian bound for missionary work in
America and in England for a few months. They
instantly became friends, and fell into theological
discussion. Bohler (who talked with Wesley in
Latin, as he spoke no English) argued that true faith
in Christ would always produce two things: mas-
tery over sin, and continuing peace arising from a
sense of being forgiven. It was, for Wesley, 'a
different gospel', and by it, he knew, 'it was clear
I had not faith'.

Bohler became friendly with both Wesley brothers, though he considered John to be the most
spiritually open; there were many conversations
between them. But John still did not fully understand Bohler's gospel, and when news reached him
in late February that Charles, whose health was still
fragile, was in Oxford and near to death he once
again in an agony of remorse flung himself into
promises of a more upright life. From now on, he
vowed, he would never laugh again and every
conversation would 'tend to the glory of God'.

He found Charles on the road to recovery, and
Peter Bohler sitting with him. The next day, discussing with Bohler again, he ran out of arguments.
In a sudden flash of illumination he realised that he
simply did not possess faith. He resolved to abandon dependence on his own works and to pray
ceaselessly for 'justifying, saving faith, a full reli-

ance on the blood of Christ shed for *me*, a trust in
him, as *my* Christ, as *my* sole justification, sanctification and redemption'. Wesley had finally begun
to find an answer to Spangenberg's probing questions of over two years earlier.

One matter troubled him. Now that he knew he
did not have faith – was, indeed, actively *seeking*
faith – ought he to go on preaching? And if so, about
what? He consulted Bohler.

'Preach faith *till* you have it,' advised his friend.
'And then, *because* you have it, you *will* preach
faith.'

Thus on 6 May 1738 Wesley began for the first
time to preach 'this new doctrine' of salvation by
faith.

THE first person to whom he preached it was a
condemned criminal named Clifford who was being held in Oxford Gaol awaiting execution. Several days later Wesley set out for Manchester on
pastoral business in the company of Charles Kinchin,
one of the Oxford 'methodists'; Kinchin was now
a follower of Whitefield and had already embraced
the doctrine of free, unearned grace. All the way
north they preached salvation by faith to anybody
who would listen, with results that often surprised
Wesley; though nothing prepared him for the visit
he and Kinchin made to Clifford's cell on their
return, on the day he was due to be hanged. The two

set the Prayer Book aside and prayed spontane-
ously for Clifford, who knelt with them in spiritual
turmoil.

But the condemned man got up transformed.
'He rose up, and eagerly said, "I am now ready to
die. I know Christ has taken away my sins, and there
is no more condemnation for me."' The two clergy-
men accompanied the radiant criminal in the cart to
the gallows. 'In his last moments he was the same,
enjoying a perfect peace, in confidence that he was
"accepted in the beloved".'

In April the Wesleys took lodgings in London
and continued their discussions with Peter Bohler.
The argument had now moved on from the question
of faith, which Wesley conceded he had yet to find,
to whether conversion might be granted instantane-
ously, to the worst of sinners as well as to the most
morally upright of citizens. How valid was Clifford's
conversion? Was there no place for the years of
obedience and self-discipline?

At Bohler's insistence the Wesleys read Scripture after Scripture, discovering to their consterna-
tion that the Bible appeared to teach that many had
become Christians by instantaneous conversion
from their sins. John suggested that this was a
phenomenon restricted to the early church. Bohler
produced witnesses, friends who testified that they
had experienced an immediate awareness of forgiveness and acceptance by God. In an emotional
conversation Wesley capitulated. He had no further

quarrel with Bohler. He could only plead: 'Lord, I believe. Help thou my unbelief!'

'Should I not *now* refrain from teaching others?' he asked Bohler.

'No,' counselled the other. 'Do not hide in the earth the talent God has given you.'

John and Charles disagreed about what Charles called 'The new faith', and there was at least one public argument between them on the subject of instantaneous conversion when both declared themselves deeply offended. But for John it was a turning-point. His head, at least, had made its peace with God. His soul would have to wait a little longer.

PETER Bohler's departure from England for America was imminent. On 1 May the Wesleys, their host James Hutton and a few others held the first meeting of a new Society that Bohler had recommended should be established. It met in Fetter Lane, and was to provide mutual encouragement, confession and prayer. The rules noted by Wesley in his journal were quite different to those of the Holy Club; this was a fellowship designed to encourage faith, not to monitor religious observances.

Charles had a long conversation with Bohler on 3 May, the day before the Moravian was to leave. He was ill: the pleurisy which had almost killed him before was back. After Bohler's departure he was visited by a brazier, a Mr Bray who 'knew nothing but Christ'. To the sick and depressed Charles, Bray seemed to be God's provision to take the place of the absent Bohler, and he accepted an invitation to move his accommodation to Bray's home in Little Britain off Aldersgate Street near St Paul's. It was at that house on the day of Pentecost that Charles, in the words of the message that was sent to John, 'found rest to his soul'. He had had a visit from his brother during the day. John was very depressed, but the brothers sang a hymn to the Holy Spirit and prayed together, and after John left Charles began to pray fervently that on this Whit Sunday the Holy Spirit would come to him. Later, drifting off to sleep, he heard a voice: 'In the name of Jesus of Nazareth, arise, and believe, and thou shalt be healed of all thy infirmities.' It was Bray's sister, longing to give Charles spiritual comfort but feeling utterly inadequate to do anything other than quote Scripture.

On hearing the words, Charles fully and completely accepted what Christ had done on the cross, as achieving salvation for him, Charles Wesley. The long years of self-discipline and the fiasco in Georgia were equally irrelevant; this was a sheer gift of God, undeserved and freely given.

'Who is so great a God as our God?' marvelled John Wesley as he and his friends joined the rejoicing round Charles's bed. But there was a heaviness in his own heart, and despite the prayers of his friends that he too would experience this certainty of the Holy Spirit, he left in gloom and depression.

THE next few days saw his depression develop into a crisis. Though barred from preaching in several London churches for his unpopular sermons about salvation by faith, he had no personal assurance at all. On 24 May he stepped out into the dirty, already crowded streets of the city with the words of his Greek Testament ringing in his mind: 'Thou art not far from the kingdom of God.' But he felt very far from sharing the joy of his brother, now rapidly regaining his health and revelling in his newly-found salvation. That afternoon he went into St Paul's Cathedral where he heard the anthem sung.

> Out of the deep have I called to thee, O Lord ... O Israel, trust in the Lord, for with the Lord there is mercy, and with him is plenteous redemption. And he shall redeem Israel from all his sins.

The words, like those he had read earlier, were full of comfort. He began to awaken to the possibility that God might be preparing him for some great encouragement.

That evening he was persuaded by James Hutton to attend a Moravian meeting. It was almost certainly held in Nettleton Court, an open square leading off Aldersgate Street. It was a rundown area; the booksellers who had once thrived there had moved on to nearby Paternoster Row. There was much criminal activity in such areas. In that year of 1738 fifty-two criminals were executed on Tyburn Gallows, and convictions for smuggling were numerous. Sunday trading, falling church attendance, youth crime, drunkenness and gambling all flourished in the capital. It is perhaps appropriate that Methodism, a movement that from the beginning was dedicated to charitable work and education, had its beginnings in a shabby court in a shabby London street.

Still burdened by his thoughts, Wesley entered the meeting room with Hutton to find that Martin Luther's *Preface to the Epistle to the Romans* was being read aloud; it has been suggested that the reader was William Holland, a leader in the Fetter Lane meeting. The impact on Wesley was powerful and precise: Wesley records more or less the exact minute that his spiritual eyes were opened.

> About a quarter before nine, while he was describing the change which God works in the heart through faith in Christ, I felt my heart strangely warmed. I felt I did trust in Christ, Christ alone for salvation; and an assurance was given me that he had taken away *my* sins, even *mine*, and saved *me* from the law of sin and death.

Immediately, he began to pray for his critics. Then he announced to everybody present what had happened. Even as the rejoicing began, the first of many doubts assailed him: if he truly had received faith, why was he not *overflowing* with joy? The others explained to him that conversion was a fact, but that God decided whether or not it should be accompanied by feelings.

The small fellowship took to the streets, traversing the few hundred yards to Bray's house where Charles was composing a hymn to celebrate his own conversion. He recorded the happy event in his journal:

> Towards ten, my brother was brought in triumph by a troop of our friends, and declared, 'I believe.' We sang the hymn with great joy, and parted with prayer.

The hymn was almost certainly 'Where shall my wandering soul begin?', which concludes:

> For you the Prince of Glory died.
> *Believe*, and all your guilt's forgiven;
> Only believe – and yours is heaven.

THERE has been much discussion about whether 24 May 1738 was the date of John Wesley's conversion. Some suggest that he was converted earlier and that the 'Aldersgate experience' merely added an emotional dimension to his faith. Others point to the fact that he rarely referred to the event afterwards, which they take to imply that he repudiated it. Others point to the waves of doubt that buffeted

him in the weeks, months and years that followed:
surely, they argue, this means that the experience
did not last. Still others argue that Wesley's coming
to faith was a gradual process in which no single
event or date in the calendar can be reckoned to be
the decisive moment.

Yet the fact remains that Wesley appears to have
been of the opinion that 24 May 1738 *was* the
crucial moment in his life. When he organised his
journal for publication – a process which involved
careful arrangement of the material to achieve
maximum edification of his readers – he not only
gave the Aldersgate experience prominence but
prefaced it with a survey of his spiritual life up to
that point. The break with the Moravians that came
later might be one reason why the episode is only
briefly referred to afterwards; and the painful recording of his doubts and depressions is logical,
given his desire to portray the human pilgrimage as
an ongoing encounter with a personal God. Indeed
Luke Tyerman, his early biographer, argues that
the Moravians taught Wesley faulty knowledge as
well as saving knowledge, and that this may well
have accounted itself for his swings of mood and
waves of doubt as he began to sift through the
dramatic experiences through which he had passed.

What is remarkable in the conversion of the
Wesleys is the way that its history is recorded in
such detail. The journals of both provide not only a
fascinating portrait of the psychology of conver-

sion, but also a record of grace taking root in the
human soul. The Oxford years provided John Wesley with an intellectual heritage and a religious
resolve that were to be essential components of his
future faith, even though they were not enough on
their own to give him the peace or the salvation for
which he yearned. His missionary service stripped
him of any illusion that he was spiritually faultless,
but it was during this period of abysmal failure that
God brought him first into contact with the Moravians. The role of godly individuals in pointing
others to Christ is illustrated by such figures as
Spangenberg, Bohler and Bray; and the success
that his preaching met with while he knew he did
not himself possess the faith he was offering indicates that the word of God does not depend on its
speakers to be effective in God's purposes.

WESLEY never left the Church of England: the
denomination of Methodism was founded after his
death. In the course of his life he travelled thousands of miles, preached continuously for fifty-
three years, read thousands of books, wrote dozens
himself, and oversaw welfare and education schemes
that transformed British society. His attractive personality and strong preaching style drew crowds to
him, not least when he took to 'field-preaching'
when the parish churches were closed to him. He
confronted many of the major figures of his day,

5

Dr Livingstone Returns Home
The First Furlough, 1856-1858

His books made him wealthy. He had discovered the African interior and made epic journeys. The public poured money into funds set up in his name; when he preached, congregations sometimes stormed the pulpit in their desire to seize his hand; once he was almost crushed to death by an enthusiastic crowd in London. Several learned societies presented him with their gold medal, cities made him their freeman, honorary degrees were awarded him, and Queen Victoria granted him an audience.

During the sixteen months of his first visit home (1856-58), after fifteen years in Africa, Dr David Livingstone found himself a public hero to a degree that no evangelical missionary had ever experienced before. It is characteristic of the Livingstone phenomenon that the adoration was not primarily for his missionary work, but for his achievements as an explorer. When he left England in 1840 to work as a missionary among the Bechuana, in the region to the north of the Cape Colony at Africa's southernmost tip, the African interior was virtually unknown territory to Europeans; it was an expanse of unmapped land interrupted only occasionally by

the activities of slave traders, other commercial
venturers and missionaries.

Many of Livingstone's biographers have cited
one of those missionaries, Robert Moffat, as the
person who inspired him to go to Africa. But it is
now known that Livingstone's mind was made up
long before he met Moffat, though the older man
was to be a very strong influence upon him, and
certainly pointed him to Bechuana territory. Moffat,
also a Scot (and later to become Livingstone's
father-in-law), had arrived in Cape Town in 1817 as
a missionary with the London Missionary Society,
and had gone north to work among the Hottentots.
In the 1820s he worked among the Bechuanas in
education, biblical and other translation and diplo-
macy. By 1839 when he returned to England he had
already made the first of many later visits to the
Matabele tribe. In London in 1840 Livingstone met
Moffat and his wife at a boarding house for missionaries in Aldersgate. Besides encouraging his
desire to be a missionary, they gave him gloomy
warnings that going to Africa as a bachelor would
probably lead to loneliness and frustration.

LIVINGSTONE was no stranger to hardship and was
used to mastering frustration; he had lived with
poverty all his life. Born in 1813 in Blantyre, near
Glasgow, he was one of seven children. The family
lived in a single room in a teeming Blantyre slum,

without water, hygiene and sanitation. David and his two brothers had to work in the cotton mill. He started there at the age of ten, his working week consisting of six exhausting twelve-and-a-half hour days, enduring sweltering heat and occasional cruelty, risking serious injury as he and his contemporaries clambered among the machinery to repair weaknesses and faults in the cotton.

Incredibly, a small group of child workers attended a night school for two hours after the long day's labours. By far the most dedicated pupil was David, who had already been taught to read and write by his father and was now determined to master Latin. The story of his childhood is a remarkable record of sheer guts. Later, many dubious legends of his childhood piety were to circulate; but the popular image of the studious teenager, ridiculed by his work mates, balancing a Latin textbook precariously on the frame of a vibrating mill machine is authentic.

His home was deeply religious. His father, Neil Livingstone, was a total abstainer (though David's mother was fond of smoking a clay pipe) who disapproved of frivolous activities, swearing and secular literature; he was a rigorous Calvinist with a strong doctrine of election. When David developed an interest in science and toyed with an ambition to become a doctor, Neil Livingstone disapproved strongly, saying that the only scientific employment Christians could pursue with a

clear conscience was one that served some specifically Christian purpose.

By the time David's teenage years ended he was
still working at the Blantyre mill and was spiritually far from at peace. Then a book – *The Philosophy of a Future State*, by Scottish nonconformist
minister Thomas Dick – convinced him that science was not incompatible with faith, and his father
moved his own church affiliation from institutional
Calvinism to a much freer, Congregational system.
He and David attended lectures by Dr Wardlaw the
Congregationalist, and among the members of the
Livingstone's new Congregational Church were
educated and wealthy men like the Christian indus-
trialist Henry Drummond, who regularly corre-
sponded with American theologians such as Charles
Finney. Both father and son were soon influenced
by American evangelicalism and also by a new
mood that was sweeping through Scottish church life.

At twenty-one David caught a vision for missionary work, mainly through the story of the China
missionary Karl Gutzlaff, who was at that time
issuing an appeal for medical missionaries. In medicine he recognised an opportunity to use his love of
science in the service of Christianity: in 1836 with
his father's blessing he entered Anderson's College, Glasgow, as a medical student. He saved the
considerable fees out of his small wages at the mill,
and worked there during the holidays to keep himself.

Modern 'debunkers' have seized on weaknesses

in Livingstone's personality, often in an understandable desire to counter-balance the hysterical adulation that he received in his lifetime. The rough edges of his character were noted by at least one unsympathetic tutor who ought to have been more understanding of Livingstone's circumstances, and they are certainly obvious when one reads about his relationships to his family. But his childhood achievements are widely recognised. By burning determination, dogged hard work and natural abilities, he broke free of the drudgery of the mills, overcame the early influence of a strict and domineering father, and fulfilled ambitions which many young people starting life with far greater advantages might have abandoned as too challenging.

In August 1838 he left Scotland to join the London Missionary Society, founded almost half a century earlier as an interdenominational Society both in membership and in practice. Between 1795 and 1845 the Society sent out 475 missionaries. It placed considerable responsibility on missionaries to use their own initiative, and left them free to choose whatever form of church government appeared to be appropriate in the missionary situation in which their workers found themselves. This pioneering attitude to denominationalism was only partially successful and before long the Society was effectively the missionary arm of the Congre-

gational Church – a denomination that had been a
very positive influence in the Livingstone family
already. David was accepted and given an unusually thorough theological training, which may have
been in recognition of what he had already shown
himself capable.

His first choice of mission field was not Africa
but China, because of the inspiring accounts of
Gutzlaff and the evident effectiveness of medical
missionaries in that country. But in 1839 the First
Opium War between Britain and China broke out
which was to last for three years; the London
Missionary Society decided to temporarily stop
sending missionaries there (paradoxically the Treaty
of Nanking which ended the war marked the beginning of an unprecedented missionary outreach to
China). When they suggested the West Indies to
Livingstone as an alternative, he argued that it was
by then too civilised a region; instead he proposed
South Africa, a suggestion that the Society accepted, six months before he met Moffat, and
proceeded to organise further training for him.

Another event that was to help form his vision
for Africa was his attendance in London at a meeting of the Society for the Extinction of the Slave
Trade and for the Civilisation of Africa. A speaker
named Thomas Buxton (whom William Wilberforce, approaching old age, had nominated as his
successor in his great crusade to destroy the slave
trade) argued that the best counter to slavery was to

develop European-style commerce to enable the
Africans to market their own goods. Livingstone
was deeply impressed, though Buxton's views were
unpopular with the majority of missionaries, who
considered trade to be an unspiritual and dishon-
ourable enterprise for a missionary. But Livingstone was open to any solution to the evil of slavery,
for which his hatred was no doubt fuelled by his
own childhood experiences in the Blantyre mills.

His vision to go to Africa now confirmed and
reinforced, he spent the rest of his time in Britain
completing his studies, recovering from a failed
romance, and practising preaching – a task made
more difficult by his ineffective manner and a
minor deformity in his throat which later had to be
dealt with by surgery. One of his last engagements
was a November meeting at Albion Chapel,
Finsbury, at which he was ordained as a Congregational minister.

He sailed for Cape Town in December 1840, and
arrived after a three-month voyage. In July 1841 he
started work at Robert Moffatt's mission station at
Kuruman, but like Moffat before him felt the pull of
the unexplored Interior. Moffat's well-known plea,
that he had sometimes seen 'in the morning sun, the
smoke of a thousand villages where no missionary
had ever been', turned out to be poetic licence, and
the only way to reach the unreached peoples was to
push further into the Interior. Moffat remained at
Kuruman where he devoted much of his time to

translation and agriculture, laying foundations upon which much that came later would be built.

From 1843 to 1853 the Livingstones worked among the Tswana, where David's educational and medical labours met with more success than his missionary efforts; only one convert is recorded, that of the Bechuana chief Sechele. Livingstone's target was not, however, converts as such; he often argued that the aim of missionary work ought not to be to accumulate lists of converts, but to achieve 'the widest possible diffusion of Christian truth and principles', so creating a favourable environment for the gospel to flourish.

Although sceptics have sometimes written off Livingstone's achievements as a missionary, it is striking how frequently his methods and strategies reflect modern thinking. The early association in his mind, for example, between missionary work and commerce has often been used as grounds for criticising him. It is certainly true that Livingstone's Christianised version of Victorian commercial imperialism owed much to his early reading among secular thinkers. Yet modern missionary and relief strategy would tend to support him in some significant ways. For example, the organisation Traidcraft helps small communities in the Third World to find Western markets for local craft products. Another Christian organisation, in India, sponsors the building of warehouses in agricultural villages, thereby enabling farmers to store produce and sell it when market prices are high. Previously they had to sell at harvest time to repay bank loans, causing a glutted market and sustaining a cycle of poverty. Yet another Christian charity, this time in Pakistan, administers a rolling fund that provides capital grants for building commercial property on unused church land. The buildings are then rented to large companies. The income pays back the loan (which is then used to fund other, similar projects) and subsequently funds a variety of local church projects.

Money is not the key to spiritual fulfilment. The poet Tennyson's vision was of a future in which commerce would usher in a global utopia:

For I dipt into the future, far as human eye could see,
Saw the Vision of the world, and all the wonder that would be;
Saw the heavens fill with commerce, argosies of magic sails,
Pirates of the purple twilight, dropping down with costly bales ...
Till the war-drum throbb'd no longer, and the battle flags were
                                                                    furl'd
In the Parliament of man, the Federation of the world.[1]

Tennyson's words, written at the same time that Livingstone arrived in Cape Town, reflect a sub-Christian version of a millennialism that did in fact form part of Livingstone's Christian beliefs. But wisely used, money has often freed people from exploitation, in both the nineteenth century and our own; and modern liberation theologians are by no means the only people who have pointed out that poverty, besides being less than God's will for human beings, is also a stumbling-block to their spiritual fulfilment.

It would be dangerous, in any case, to simplify the association between evangelism and commerce that Livingstone advocated. He was proposing not an exploitation of the African people but the development of an indigenous cotton industry. And though Britain would certainly benefit from this new source of materials, it would mean that she was no longer dependent on cotton that had come from the slave plantations. Livingstone saw the opening up of a new commercial market as one of the legitimate rewards by which Britain's motives in Africa would be given divine blessing, but like Wilberforce before him he regarded 'legitimate trade' as one of the prime weapons against slavery. It is a measure of how his thinking developed that Karl Gutzlaff, whose example had first inspired Livingstone to go to the mission field, was unavoidably implicated in the Chinese opium trade and could by no stretch of the imagination be called a legitimate trader.

Similarly, Livingstone's desire to diffuse Christian principles has sometimes been seen either as weak evangelism or as an admission of failure. But it has points in common with modern thinking on 'pre-evangelism'; the conviction that in order to become Christians people often (though not always) need first to be brought in their thinking to a place from which they can properly understand the truth of the gospel. It is certainly the case that churches which today flourish in the southern and central African continent have acknowledged a very great debt to the pioneering work of David Livingstone.

In January 1845 Livingstone married Mary, Robert Moffat's daughter. She was to have a marriage that was probably quite unlike any she might have expected. She accompanied her husband on many of his epic journeys (often despite strong protests from her mother to David), eventually dying in 1862 of fever at the end of the Zambesi Expedition. There is a touching deathbed scene recorded, in which a distraught Livingstone makes a final attempt to remove the spiritual doubts that had troubled Mary for years. The anecdote contrasts with the terse, unromantic and frequently derogatory comments Livingstone made about his wife in correspondence through the years, but has a ring of truth about it that suggests that Livingstone may have rarely allowed his emotions to be involved in his letters.

In Bechuanaland Livingstone found a population organised tribally, living in towns and villages; as they were a mainly farming people, this meant much movement of livestock in search of new pastures and additional problems for missionary workers trying to establish enduring relationships

with the people. The pace of life and the local
customs were completely different to the British
pattern, and there was no significant trade or market economy at all. The Africans struggled to make
a livelihood in a dry and difficult land, but did not
see the arrival of technologically sophisticated and
relatively prosperous Westerners as a reason to
change their way of life. They were, too, a polyga-
mous society, and their attitude to property was
complex and thoroughly non-Western.

Moffat and Livingstone lived long before the
debates over 'contextualising' the gospel; and
though William Carey (1761-1834) had laid many
of the foundations for modern mission thinking,
another half century and more would elapse before
such seminal works as Dan Crawford's *Thinking
Black* (1912) would emphasise the importance of
thinking oneself into the African mentality and
seeking to understand African culture as a prelude
to evangelism (though Crawford placed a far higher
importance on individual conversion than did Livingstone). In the early 1840s, British missionaries
tended to possess an image of the native African as
utterly depraved, morally corrupt, and socially
primitive. Polygamy was seen as unrestrained sexual excess, though in many cultures it was rigorously administered by convention and local law. Nudi-
ty was taken as a special evidence of depravity so
that for some, evangelising Africa was tantamount
to clothing the continent.

It has been said of Livingstone, however, that he discovered 'not only Africa but the African'. David L. Edwards comments: 'His work was simply to get to know and to love Africa and the Africans, recording his observations with meticulous care.'[2] The means by which he did so were his great journeys, across the deserts of the Kalahari and deep into the north country.

In 1849 he made his first great discovery, Lake Ngami. With two companions he succeeded where others had failed, largely because the team understood the nature of African deserts and seasons. The discovery was welcomed by the London Missionary Society, who realised that it would prompt public generosity, and the Royal Geographical Society made him a (very small) financial grant.

In 1853 Livingstone embarked on 'the greatest journey of exploration ever made by one man'. It took him from Cape Town to the Zambesi, on a journey to find a route into the Interior that avoided hostile Boer territory. Seeking a better route, he then followed the Zambesi across the whole continent to the Indian Ocean. On his travels he discovered a magnificent waterfall which he named after his Queen. The journey had been almost 2,500 miles. By the time he returned to Britain his name was a household word.

DURING 1857 Livingstone addressed audiences of both Oxford and Cambridge undergraduates. He presented them with a stirring challenge to missionary work. 1859 saw the formation of the Oxford and Cambridge Universities Mission as a direct consequence of his appeals, and the new Society committed itself to working in Central Africa. It had been a powerful appeal. In 1857 Livingstone told a Cambridge audience,

> I know that in a few years I shall be cut off in that country which is now open; do not let it be shut again! I go back to Africa to try to make an open path for commerce and Christianity; do you carry out the work which I have begun. I leave it to you.

The 'open path' he was talking about was the Zambesi, the great water highway that drove deep into the heart of Central Africa. It was perhaps Livingstone's greatest single contribution to the theory of mission that a river could be a highway; not simply a road upon which the gospel could travel, but an economic unit, the cohering focus of a commercial structure. Around an explored Zambesi, Western outposts would appear; trading posts, mission stations, schools. Settlers would come from Christian Europe, drawn by the beauty of the territory and the plentifulness of natural resources. The Africans would be able to develop, to create a Western-style economy. And two things would flow from this: firstly, the slave trade would wither away, extinguished by the new prosperity of the Africans; and secondly, the churches would be the centre of a virile, growing Christianity.

It has been suggested that Livingstone's missionary zeal was a poor second to his desire to be an explorer. It is certainly true that there was in Livingstone a mind and an imagination deeply moved by the sights he saw, and drawn by the challenge and wonder of the unknown territories. But it was the other way round; the explorations were merely the means to penetrate the dark continent, so that others could come afterwards with the gospel.

He went back to Africa in 1858. His passion for exploration and his enthusiasm for promoting commerce, though both were the fruit of a profound evangelistic urgency, had led to a parting of the ways between Livingstone and the London Missionary Society. He had announced this to the Society in October 1857, having already entered into discussions with the British government to allow him to be appointed a British consul. The following March, the Zambesi Expedition set sail under Livingstone's leadership. It was intended to realise his great dream of an 'open path for commerce and Christianity', by assessing whether the river was navigable.

The project was thwarted from the outset. The Portuguese who ruled the territories of the Lower

Zambesi saw no reason to do the expedition any favours, and Livingstone had seriously underestimated the navigability of the river, which defeated his purpose-built steamer completely at the Cabora Bassa Rapids. It was a heavy blow, for apart from the failure of the original vision (and the loss of public prestige), the sheer difficulty of the river meant that the Zambesi could never become the 'open path' he had wanted it to be. He made a detour northward, away from the Zambesi, along the Shire River to Lake Malawi of which he was the discoverer. There, in a populated and rural region, he might have been able to establish a centre of European commerce that would have dented the slave trade by removing the need for Africans to sell their own people to survive. But the British government ordered the expedition home in 1863.

It had been a time of great discouragement for Livingstone. Abandoning the Zambesi was, for him, abandoning 'God's highway'. Relations with his fellow team-members – difficult at the best of times – were no better on this expedition. The bishop who had been sent out by the Oxford and Cambridge mission died of dysentery in 1862. And the final blow was the loss of Mary Livingstone, buried under a baobab tree in Shupanga near the mouth of the great river that had dominated their lives. She was forty-one years old.

THE adulation of his earlier furlough was largely absent when he came home for the second time in 1864-65. He had lost credibility with the government. He returned to Africa in 1866 as an unpaid consul, exploring the virgin territories between the Malawi and Tanganyika lakes. His declared aim was to discover the source of the Nile; he also wanted to expose the Arab slave trade and thus to bring it to an end. The reports he sent back to Britain were a very considerable factor in the global abolition of slavery that followed not long after his death.

He disappeared from public view, and it was not known whether or not he was still alive. In 1871 a journalist, H. M. Stanley, sent out by the *New York Herald* to find Livingstone, had a legendary meeting with the explorer at Ujiji in November 1871. Livingstone steadfastly refused Stanley's pleas for him to return home, saying that God still had work for him to do in Africa. Stanley returned home unsuccessful, and Livingstone continued with his travels.

He died, a solitary European among Africans, in the village of Chitambo in May 1873. The story of his last journey to the coast, as his African friends carried his body on a hazardous route to ship their beloved missionary home to be buried in Britain, stirred the hearts of the public. Livingstone died a greater public hero than he had ever been before. He was laid to rest in Westminster Abbey. Among the mourners was a single African, sent by the missionaries, 'as a fund-raising exercise', comments Tim Jeal wryly.[3]

The sixty Africans who had risked so much to bring Livingstone's body to the coast, and some of whom had given their master several years' faithful service, received a small cash payment for their trouble. The following year the Royal Geographical Society produced a medal to commemorate that last trip, but by then the sixty men were scattered. Hardly any of them received the medal. From the British government they received nothing at all.

IN many ways, Livingstone remains a conundrum of missionary history, especially for those who want to count souls to evaluate missionary success. Many of his ideas were idiosyncratic and some distasteful, though he has fared less well in public esteem than, for example, C. T. Studd, whose views (for example) on the role of the husband in marriage were similarly severe. And though his central conviction that commerce was the best way to prepare a nation for Christian evangelism was flawed (he was somewhat uncritical of Western affluence, for example), the principle – as we have already seen – is one that is present in much groundbreaking missionary work today.

Perhaps because he is a complex figure, Livingstone has been a favourite target for 'debunkers' since his death: sometimes not entirely unhelpfully, for it is a useful exercise to scrutinise great heroes of the faith to check whether our adulation actually diminishes the work of grace God achieved in their lives. But some recent studies have turned again to his strengths and his achievements, particularly as the Christian history of Central Africa begins to be written and Livingstone's contribution to be properly assessed.

He was a man of immense personal motivation, whether one considers his early childhood and education, or the huge courage of his pioneering exploration of Africa. His view of evangelism can be better appreciated today, when so many African churches acknowledge his contribution. His gifts of communication and inspiration challenged thousands to look to Africa as a place to serve God, and his motivation as an explorer surely presents one of the more attractive faces of colonial history. And his view of Africa mission was some years ahead of its time, not least in its conviction that the greatest threat to African stability was tribalism – a view that has been confirmed many times in twentieth-century African history.

Yet though he was complex, his life may be best explained by his simplest characteristics. Why, having been fêted and made wealthy during his first furlough, did he go back to a life of danger, with no guarantee of financial reward? And why, having returned to Britain as a failure, did he then go back to the continent where he had seen his dreams perish?

One reason is surely that he was a man possessed by a vision; a man who carried a river in his head. But much more than that, Britain's greatest Africa explorer was also one of her greatest anti-slavery fighters. He loved the African people and wanted above all to bring the slave trade to an end. He hoped to do so by offering them better trade, and by so doing to open doors for the gospel. Those who gleefully produce his one known convert as proof of his failure may be looking in the wrong place. His enduring memorial may be better found in the thriving settlements and developing industries and agriculture that grew up, after his death, in the territories bordering the river, and in the people that he loved.

Notes

1. Alfred, Lord Tennyson, 'Locksley Hall', included in *Poems* (1842).
2. David L. Edwards, *Christian England* (Collins, 1981-1984, repr. 1989), part iii p.329.
3. Tim Jeal, *Livingstone* (Heinemann, 1973), p.369.

6

Dwight L. Moody
The British Campaigns

In 1867 an American travelling shoe-salesman from Boston, Dwight Lyman Moody by name, visited England to meet his wife's relatives. What they thought of their new kinsman-by-marriage is not known, but he was certainly a remarkable individual. His looks – he was a short, barrel-chested man whose compelling slate-grey eyes were set in a round face framed in a flowing beard – set him apart, and so did his voice, effortlessly commanding attention whether he was speaking loudly or softly.

His story was as striking as his appearance. Moody was a classic example of the 'rough diamond', raising himself from poverty and lack of education, through hard work and business flair. He was born in 1837 in a farming community in Northfield, Massachusetts, a place that was important to him throughout his life. His father died when Moody was four years old leaving his efficient but impoverished mother to bring up her large family on her own. Dwight (he hardly ever used the name) received a rudimentary education, a fact that he constantly regretted as an adult – though he was famous for his cheerful acknowledgement of his atrocious spelling and punctuation. Like many successful businessmen before and since, he compensated for lack of formal advantages by boundless energy, common sense and an outstanding head for business.

He entered the shoe-selling trade in 1854, and joined the Young Mens' Christian Association to improve his social life. His religious upbringing had been unorthodox, for his mother was a Unitarian. Her brothers, however, were Christians, and Moody attended their church in Boston. Not long after starting work he became a Christian when his Sunday School teacher explained to him that Jesus loved him and wished to be loved in return. It was an uncomplicated experience marked by great joy – 'the following day the old sun shone a good deal brighter than it ever had before ... It seemed to me I was in love with all creation' – and an inability to talk meaningfully about exactly what he perceived his conversion to have been about. His difficulty in giving an articulate testimony led to the deacons of his uncles' church refusing to admit him to membership, but they relented twelve months later, unable to resist Moody's plain sincerity and zeal.

A year later he moved to Chicago, a thriving and expanding city where his career took off and he became prosperous. He began to be active in evangelistic work among deprived children living in the slums, work in which he found his lack of formal education and theological skills more than compensated for by an attractive speaking style and a gift for seizing the children's attention and imagination as he told them Bible stories. A Sunday School which he founded grew to become a local church. Soon his skills in administration were recognised by others, and his preaching authority and the general climate of revival current in America at that time – the 'Second Evangelical Awakening' – helped to bring him to public notice. Before long it was clear that Moody's future lay in the pulpit.

He continued as a salesman for several years and made money. His life revolved round his energetic evangelistic work in Chicago and the rural life to which he liked to escape back in Northfield. Those who knew him at this time described him as an ambitious and able salesman, but lacking the 'killer instinct'. In 1860, realising that he had to make a choice between the two main interests of his life, he retired from business to become a full-time unpaid evangelist. By 1864 he was involved in outreach to immigrant families. His reputation as a preacher was enhanced by his election to the Presidency of the Chicago YMCA. During the American Civil War he served as a lay chaplain, though he was never ordained.

His marriage in 1862 to the Englishwoman, Emma Revell, and the birth in due course of their daughter and two sons, created a happy and supportive home life that sustained Moody throughout his strenuous ministry. It was said that Emma was the perfect foil to Moody. Her calm trust in God and winsome personality complemented, and took the rough edges off, Moody's more extrovert and aggressive manner which in Chicago had earned him the nickname 'Crazy Moody'. Nevertheless his reputation as a preacher continued to grow.

WHEN Moody arrived in Britain in 1867 he found that his reputation had gone before him; the YMCA was an international organisation and his American evangelistic work was well known among British evangelicals. In retrospect it can be seen as a significant visit both in the long and the short term. In Dublin he met Harry Moorhouse who had been a thief; Moorhouse convinced Moody that he must preach the love of God rather than God's wrath, and a change of emphasis appeared in Moody's preaching, though fear of eternal punishment and the awful destiny of the wicked was never entirely absent from his preaching. In the short-term, seeds were sown in that first visit that were to grow when the Moodys returned in 1872; it was not supposed to be a preaching visit, but he did preach and in consequence three separate groups asked him to consider coming to Britain for an extended preaching tour.

It was a moment of crucial change in Moody's life. In 1871 the Great Fire of Chicago had swept through the city. In its path of destruction were the YMCA building, the churches with which he was involved, and his own home. In the winter of that year he went to New York to raise funds to rebuild them, and while there had a deep spiritual experience.

> 'I can only say that God revealed Himself to me, and I had such an experience of His love that I had to ask Him to stay His hand.' .... Crazy Moody became Moody the man of God.[1]

The fund-raising expedition left him physically exhausted and spiritually yearning to find God's direction for his future. With all that Moody had worked for in Chicago now in ashes, what was he to do next? In England in 1872 he met Henry Varley, a butcher, who remarked, 'The world has yet to see what God will do with a man fully consecrated to him' – a speculation which Moody resolved would find its answer in his own life.

IN 1870 he had met a singer, Ira D. Sankey, who had not had any musical training but possessed a natural singing gift and a fine voice. At Moody's invitation Sankey had become a familiar contributor to the worship in the church that had grown from the Sunday School work, and the two often worked together in evangelism. When Moody decided to accept the invitation to go back to Britain in 1872 for the preaching tour, it was natural that he would ask Sankey to go with him, and typical of the strength of their family life that they should both take their families with them. Unfortunately the planning had been minimal on both sides, and the two families arrived in Liverpool in June to find that nothing had been arranged and no money raised.

The YMCA came to the rescue, for they had invited Moody previously to speak in York. Moody, who had not yet decided whether to accept, did so now. The venerable cathedral city was a forbidding place to begin the tour, but the meetings went well and an invitation to preach in Newcastle followed. Then in its industrial heyday, Newcastle had much in common with Chicago and the pair were well received. But it was not until the Americans reached Edinburgh at the end of the year that the first major public excitement began. During 1874 they travelled throughout Scotland, where the impact of their preaching not only led to large numbers of people becoming Christians, but also prompted local Christians to launch their own evangelistic activities.

By the time they arrived in London in March 1875, by way of Ireland and northern England, they were well-known names in the capital. After the disappointments of their arrival in England in 1873, the organisation of the London meetings was extremely effective. Careful choice of venues attracted audiences from every social stratum from the poor to the aristocracy: the former in a shelter on Bow Common, the latter at the Royal Opera House. It was said that a total of 2,500,000 flocked to listen[2], and there was a mood of revival in the city. The tour lasted until July, by which time Moody and Sankey had become enthusiastically accepted by most British evangelicals. Though there were dissenting voices and many had various reservations about aspects of the meetings, Moody steadfastly refused to answer his critics and would not be drawn into wrangling; and he had the rare gift of heading a team of local Christians, using their gifts and creating a harmonious and effective group ministry.

Moody and Sankey returned to America famous. Throughout the late 1870s they conducted evangelistic campaigns, characterised as the British campaign had been by close involvement with local churches and much encouragement by the evangelists that there should be adequate preparation before their arrival and adequate follow-up afterwards. This was such a departure from the general American practice that Moody and Sankey can be said to have laid the foundations of a campaigning tradition which found its best-known exponent in Billy Graham.

They acquired fortune as well as fame, for Sankey's hymnbook *Sacred Songs and Solos* was a national best-seller; but they refused to take any of the money for themselves and invested it in trust funds out of which a number of educational institutions were endowed. The outflowing of their pulpit ministry into social welfare and education recalls the eighteenth-century evangelical revival: Wesley, for example, involved himself in causes that would have ensured his place in history as a social reformer and educationalist, had he never entered a pulpit.

IN 1882 Moody and Sankey returned to Britain for campaigns that were to last until 1884.

The result was large numbers of the poor turning to Christianity; the rich too were touched by the preaching, notably in a mission at Cambridge University. There, Moody survived the confrontation between the sophisticated, worldly-wise students and the uneducated and badly-spoken evangelist. The Cambridge meetings profoundly influenced many who would later be prominent in church and state. Among them were the 'Cambridge Seven', who in 1885 were to relinquish their privileged positions in England to become missionaries to China.

Back in America Moody's causes included a series of conferences at Northfield designed to fire Christians with a zeal for evangelising the world. The impact of the conferences was far-reaching. In 1886 he founded the Chicago Evangelization Society, which later became the Moody Bible Institute, where people who like Moody had no formal educational qualifications could train for Christian work. Later, Moody Press was founded as a literature evangelism project. Both Institute and Press flourish today.

Moody suffered from ill health as he grew older, but he never stopped working. In a campaign in November 1899 at Kansas City his weakened heart failed, and he died on December 22. He was bedridden (which he hated) for most of his final days, surrounded by his family and receiving daily messages of sympathy and encouragement from hundreds of well-wishers. He longed to be up and preaching again, and wondered whether God might grant him a miracle; yet he spoke confidently and surely of his salvation and his longing to be with God.

Will Moody, who as Moody's son and official biographer was anxious to faithfully record every detail of the passing of the great man, wrote down many of Moody's last contemplations. Describing the funeral that followed, he noted:

Toward the close ... a striking scene occurred .... Suddenly a single ray shone through the upper window at the extreme end, opposite the platform. It fell upon the side and close to the head of the casket .... Then moving slowly as the sun descended, as though searching for its object, it fell full upon the exposed face – a halo of light from Heaven – suffusing the familiar and natural features with a brightness in

keeping with the glad heart that had throbbed in life.
The sunshine touched no other object ...[3]

It is understandable that his son's biography should
end with the kind of miraculous sign that mediaeval
scribes believed to be the appropriate way of describing the death of a saint. They saw it as a
miraculous attestation of the divine pleasure; it was
important that saints die well. Moody, who would
have found the symbolism much to his taste, would
only have accepted the title of saint if every Christian possessed it too; but he was revered by millions
and Will Moody is plainly anxious that we should
see the sunbeam (which, there is no reason to doubt,
did actually illuminate his father's face) as a sign
from God and a comfort to those who mourned him.

A better tribute to the remarkable quality of the
man, perhaps, is to be found in the eulogy by G.
Campbell Morgan with which Will Moody concludes.

Bright, cheery, and yet in dead earnest, he seemed to
make everything go before him .... I sat by his side
and watched, and began to understand the greatness
of the man, whose life was so broad that it touched
sympathetically all other phases of life. After the
evening meeting, at his invitation, I gathered with the
speakers at his house. Then for the first time I saw
him in a new role, that of the host .... In that brief stay
Moody had become more to me. Strong, tender,
considerate, from that day I more than revered him –
I loved him.[4]

MODERN assessments of Moody and Sankey's work have reached varying conclusions. Most historians agree that the British campaigns were part of a general nationwide movement of the Spirit of God rather than a catalyst that alone prompted revival. It is wrong to see Moody as a firebrand who set alight a spiritually moribund Britain, any more than the view of John Wesley as a blazing evangelical beacon in a spiritual eighteenth-century night can be sustained.

In 1875 at the time of the first campaign there were a number of evangelical cross-currents. One was the first of the annual Keswick Conventions. The Keswick movement stressed personal holiness and personal experience of God, and though not universally approved of by evangelicals was supported by some very influential figures such as Bishop Handley Moule.

Indeed, one strand of spiritual awakening was abroad from an unlikely quarter: 1875 saw the second of two series of meetings organised by Anglo-Catholic churches in London (the first had been in 1869), which aimed to provide teaching and influence people who had left the churches, to rejoin. It was a specifically Catholic rather than an evangelical model, though it did contribute the word 'mission' to the Christian vocabulary. It may be that part of the welcome that Moody received from evangelicals was due to their hope that in this gifted and popular preacher lay the antidote to

Catholic revivalism, though John Kent has drawn
attention to the fact that whereas Moody and Sankey's campaigns were heavily centred on their
personalities, the Anglo-Catholic method, drawing
on the parish system and sacramental rather than
sermon-based, placed its greatest emphasis on Christian baptism where Moody and Sankey were pleading for instantaneous conversion and an experience
of forgiveness.[5]

In this context of awakening spirituality, the
impact of the American evangelists was immense,
not least because of the extraordinary nature of a
Moody and Sankey meeting. Moody's pulpit oratory, aided by his charismatic speaking voice, was
designed to shock and move his hearers. He drew
graphic pictures of sinners who had rejected Christ
and found, too late, that they had been wrong. He
told alarming anecdotes of young people who had
gone their own way, only to perish with the dreadful
certainty of a godless eternity. Telling a congregation of a child who had been appallingly mutilated
when a train ran over his body, he assured them that
he would prefer to see his own son totally dismem-
bered rather than have him face death unsaved; and
throughout, Sankey's emotional singing, and the
harmonies and words of the hymns he sang, pressed
the claims of the gospel. Typical is the hymn
written by Robert Lowry and sung by Sankey with
great effect to a sentimental tune loaded with emotional harmonies:

> Go for my wandering boy tonight;
> Go search for him where you will;
> But bring him to me with all his blight
> And tell him I love him still ...

The aim was to bring the congregation to the point where they would voluntarily decide to turn from their sin and follow Jesus. As, indeed, many of his modern successors do, Moody was trying to force a commitment of the will.

His Calvinist critics pointed out that such a decision was as much within the sinner's power as it would have been for the hundredth sheep, pursued by the shepherd in the parable, to have found its own way home. It was the Saviour who sought out the sinner, not the other way round.

Other critics of Moody's theology have pointed to the simplicity of his teaching, a simplicity that many have felt to be dangerously misleading. For example William J. Abraham points out:

There is in [Charles Finney's] work a very pragmatic strain that is anxious to get on with the job so that theology becomes a handmaid of practice rather than an equal partner in dialogue. By the time we come to his successors, D. L. Moody and Billy Sunday, there is no serious theological substance at all. Moody is a fascinating figure who did gather around him at times scholars of considerable distinction, but his theological interests were limited in the extreme.[6]

Yet another criticism which was widely made at the

time of the campaigns was of the innovative 'enquiry room' to which those moved by the sermon and wishing to make a commitment or talk further about the gospel were invited to go. In the opinion of many, it was dangerously similar to the confessionals held after the Anglo-Catholic meetings. Even after that misunderstanding was cleared up, there were accusations that the enquiry rooms were badly supervised, that unauthorised counsellors were able to gain admittance because of inadequate security, and that those who had been officially appointed counsellors often had dubious spiritual credentials.

The problems appear to have been real ones, but Moody's achievements should not be allowed to be neutralised by what was often a reaction of unfamiliarity. For many observers in Britain, Moody and Sankey's meetings seemed theatrical and bizarre by comparison with, for example, the parish church with its solemnity, ritual and frequently short and insubstantial sermon. By contrast, the Moody and Sankey events seemed hardly to be services at all:

It is significant that the central activities are described as meetings. They were not traditional religious services; indeed detractors complained of a lack of reverence and suggested the evangelists had learned from the circus impresario P. T. Barnum. In contrast to the stiff formality, high seriousness and rather ponderous preaching usual at the time, Moody's meetings were relaxed and easy flowing, with a minimum of fuss and solemnity and a stress on participation .... Sankey and his music made a two-fold contribution to the meetings. In the first place they greatly increased congregational involvement. Critics likened it to the style of the music hall, but for many unaccustomed to the ways of churches it became an experience of worship. Secondly the songs both expressed a range of religious emotions and enabled those who sang to express them.[7]

Much of the criticism was to do with the method of conducting the meetings and the 'fragile theology' (as William Abraham puts it) of Dwight L. Moody. But there are wider implications that follow from the type of preaching that he practised. For him, every sinner was poised on the brink of the pit, and the overwhelming duty of the preacher was to convince him or her of that fact as soon as possible and provide an immediate opportunity for the sinner to repent. The church of Christ was, to change the metaphor to another that he favoured, a lifeboat pulling away from a sinking ship. All around were people struggling in an ocean that would overwhelm them if they were not snatched from the waters and pulled into the lifeboat.

It was an essentially Arminian concept, based as it was on the freedom and the responsibility of the individual human being to choose whether or not to accept Jesus' work of salvation for themselves, without the emphasis on the sovereignty of God in election and calling that a Calvinist would have required. It was a direct challenge to the will, by persuasion, to make a correct decision, and it provided a suitable emotional ambience as favourable as possible to the making of that decision. Yet among the longer-term implications were cultural as well as theological ones. If conversion was simply a matter of persuading the sinner to change his mind, then what need was there to change the whole person? And if the culture in which a sinner lived was a crumbling precipice or a treacherous sea, what good thing could there possibly be in it?

In Moody's case, such contemplations resulted in an arbitrary plundering of popular culture in search of bait which, redeemed from its doomed context, could be used to lure the sinner in (for example, Sankey's use of music-hall tunes), but without really considering the resonances and associations that some of his borrowings brought with them. Moody's crusades were a marriage of theatre and music-hall, but neither of these could be redeemed merely by altering their texts to biblical ones. The consequences for Christian church music were often horrendous, as churches later tried to recreate in their congregational singing the hushed, plaintive emotionalism of Sankey's music and the flamboyant drama of Moody's pulpit style.

The tradition of *Sacred Songs and Solos*, *Sankey's 1,200* and the hymns of the Alexander hymnals and many more survived two world wars and is still strong in some British nonconformist circles; the present writer has sung 'Hold the fort for I am coming' in a Northern Ireland congregation, and 'Come home, come home – you who are weary, come home' in a Merseyside one. The story of Christian popular music in the 1960s, too, repeats many aspects of Moody and Sankey, not least in its liking for shackling tunes such as that of the Tyrolean yodelling song 'I love to go a-wandering' to words such as 'I know that my Redeemer liveth'. Often the same underlying theological assumptions were present; that the music (and later the theatre) was of value only as a lure, that the crucial role of evangelism was to grasp the imperilled sinner on the very brink of hell.

The consequences of Moody and Sankey's work include growth of evangelical churches together with a deepening social concern in England as well as in America from evangelicals. In these respects the Moody revivals can be seen as true heirs of the evangelical revival a hundred years before. Unlike that revival, however, Moody's influence reached only a limited number of British churches, and the theological weakness of the teaching meant that no strong tradition was developed after Moody and Sankey had gone back to America.

Yet the legacy was a great one. Whole communities, such as those in his beloved Northfield, revered him in a way that seems to have left him remarkably unspoilt yet created the local support and fellowship he needed to support his educational plans. In his 'campaigns' (he used the word himself, deliberately taking it from the vocabulary of warfare) he reiterated the principle of local churches and clergy being fully involved before, during and after the campaign. And, by no means insignificantly, he established the principle of having Christians meeting for prayer during the meetings but not in the same place, seeking the blessing of God on the proceedings.

During his lifetime, it is estimated, he travelled more than a million miles and addressed more than 100,000,000 people. At an early point in his ministry, Billy Graham decided that he could take no better preacher as his model. Indeed, Moody has been explicitly credited as the founder of modern mass evangelism:

> Moody hit on the idea of combining his address with the use of a skilful singer whom he saw as playing a subordinate role. Sankey, less subordinate than Moody had expected, developed the massed choir. The outcome was modern mass evangelism proper, for the device of the choir and the popular song provided the binding element necessary if the revivalists were to control and manipulate crowds of the size which came to the Agricultural Hall.[8]

DISCUSSION of Moody's work is an ongoing subject over which much ink has been spilt. Yet at the heart of the whole phenomenon is the impulsive, rough personality who never lost his love of farming and radiated the love of God: whose effect on one English listener was, 'I could never listen to Moody without feeling the strongest desire to love and know Christ.'

The final word, then, may well be left to those who admired him for his zeal for evangelism and his simple spirituality. Here is the assessment of a writer on evangelical spirituality:

> Moody was not introspective by nature, and the well-being of his soul was affected more by the success or failure of the work than by fluctuating moods and recurring questions of the inner life. His is the spirituality of the evangelist, the Christian who is utterly captivated by the message, and whose activism on the grand scale is devotion writ large. He exemplifies the uncomplicated spirituality of the Christian extrovert, less preoccupied with the profounder notes sounded by guilt, self-doubt and spiritual restlessness.[9]

And the biographer who did most to commend him to British readers sums up Moody's life in the following words:

> No man had ever done more for the Christian cause in his generation. He had recruited for Christ many who were leaders in the next. And Moody's character, dedication, and faith had set a standard in evangelism by which those who come after are judged.[10]

Notes

1. John Pollock, *Moody Without Sankey* (1963), p.87.

2. The total attendance was claimed to be 2,530,000, but this figure did not take into account those who went more than once. John Pollock, *op. cit.* p.150, suggests that the number of people who attended Moody and Sankey's meetings in London was around 1,500,000.

3. W. R. Moody, *The Life of Dwight L. Moody* (1900), p.478.

4. *Ibid.*, p.508.

5. John Kent, *Holding the Fort* (Epworth, 1978), p.236 ff.

6. William J. Abraham, *The Logic of Evangelism* (Eerdmans, 1989), p.9.

7. B. G. Worrall, *The Making of the Modern Church: Christianity in England since 1800* (SPCK, 1988), pp. 231-2

8. John Kent, *op. cit.*, p.154.

9. James M. Gordon, *Evangelical Spirituality: from the Wesleys to John Stott* (SPCK, 1991), p.162.

10. John Pollock, 'D. L. Moody and Revival', in: John D. Woodbridge (ed.), *Great Leaders of the Christian Church* (Moody Press, 1988), p. 342.

7

Jim Elliot of Ecuador
Wheaton College, 1945-1949
The Making of a Missionary

In some of the stories told in this book, the path of self-discipline has sometimes been a quite wrong direction. John Wesley, for example, set himself rigorous standards both in his schooldays and his university career: but the 'Holy Club', though a byword for ascetic discipline and spiritual single-mindedness, never got to grips with the real problems of the human heart. It's not surprising it failed to do so, for the apostle Paul pointed out exactly the same problem long ago: 'Under Gamaliel I was thoroughly trained in the law of our fathers and was just as zealous for God as any of you are today. I persecuted the followers of this Way to their death ...' (Acts 22:3-4).

But the Bible makes it clear that what matters is one's motive. To the youthful Wesley and Saul of Tarsus, it seemed that the way to God was through pleasing him, by painfully fulfilling irksome and laborious duty. It was much later in their lives that they found that God could never be reached by human effort alone; and that because humanity had no hope of reaching up to God by their own resources and thereby winning his admiration and forgiveness, God himself had stooped down and done what humanity could not do: he had achieved reconciliation through his Son, Jesus Christ. And once that had become a reality to Wesley and Saul and millions more throughout history, they embraced self-discipline not out of necessity but out of love; not out of fear but out of gratitude and a determination to draw as close as possible to the God who had so miraculously revealed himself to them.

JIM Elliot was less than thirty years old when in 1956 he died with four companions, slaughtered in the waters of the Curary River, Ecuador by the Auca Indians to whom they had come as missionaries. His short life was marked by astonishing single-mindedness, a ruthless cutting-out of anything that might distract him from his goal: 'to know God'[1].

It was an aim that was established very early in life. He was born in 1927. His parents took their children to church from the time they were six weeks old, and every day their father (who worked as an evangelist) read the Bible to them and prayed with them. When he was six years old, Jim told his mother, 'I'm saved now.' He immediately began telling his friends about Jesus, often preaching to them from the lawn swing; and the constant stream of visitors to the home – many of them missionaries on leave – gave the Elliot children important lessons in hospitality and adaptability as well as many opportunities to meet people from different walks of life and to hear about God's work in other parts of the world.

Jim's childhood was packed with activity and interests. He had a flair for art and an enthusiasm for agriculture and farming. Friends from those days recall his energy and commitment: one, describing Jim hurtling into school late on his bicycle, recalls a 'picture of speed, fury and recklessness'.

In 1941 Jim entered high school, where he majored in architectural drawing and displayed a remarkable range of gifts and abilities. He was direct and unabashed about his Christian faith, always praying before meals, carrying a Bible with him everywhere, and taking every opportunity to talk about Jesus and the Bible to anybody who could be persuaded to listen. He was recognised as one of the ablest public speakers in the school, he was also a keen sportsman and he loved the outdoors. But he was an unusual student even at high school, in at least two ways: though a popular and successful student, he chose not to have a steady girlfriend, though he would certainly have been regarded as a popular catch; and he was reluctant to allow his sporting and outdoor activities to extend over a full weekend, because he was strongly committed to the Gospel Hall he attended.

Though he was a respected and accomplished student, he never became class president. Elisabeth Elliot suggests two reasons for this. One was his pacifist stance, modelled on the principle of non-resistance which he felt Jesus had conclusively demonstrated on the cross; to hold such a view in college during the Second World War meant attracting a good deal of criticism, especially as he was not reluctant to discuss his views. Another factor that might well have permanently damaged his chances of becoming president was his invitation to Mun Hope, a young Chinese preacher, to address the school assembly. Mun Hope's uncompromisingly biblical sermon on sin and punishment, delivered to the whole staff and student body, was received with some perplexity and resentment.

Jim entered Wheaton College, Illinois, in 1945. He arrived absolutely confident that Wheaton was God's choice for him, and he was sure that God would supply the necessary funds to see him through – faith which was justified, for his college fees and living expenses were all covered for his four years at the College.

Wheaton College had been founded as a liberal arts college in 1860. Under the leadership of Jonathan Blanchard and his son Charles who succeeded him as president, it rapidly established itself as an institution committed to the fundamental doctrines of the Christian faith. Over the 135 years of its existence, Wheaton College has stood for the intellectual credibility of the Christian faith and for academic excellence. Today, members of faculty are to be found in a wide range of secular academic enterprises where their presence demonstrates that a strong commitment to biblical Christianity is anything but incompatible with a willingness to confront the intellectual challenges of the day.

Wheaton in 1945 required its students (and also faculty and staff) to commit themselves to abstaining from smoking, playing cards, alcohol, attending theatres and a number of other activities that were considered dangerous for spiritual welfare, and to sign an agreement to do so.[2] While this did not turn the college into a monastery, the appeal to self-discipline undoubtedly appealed to Jim, who as a freshman was characterised by a singleness of purpose even more intense than that which had marked his high school years. He planned his college life like an athlete planning a major race, or – to use an image in 2 Timothy 2:4 of which Jim was fond – like a soldier marching off to war. He analysed his primary objectives and set out to eliminate everything else.

He took up wrestling, which seemed to be a good preparation for a life of Christian service and had Bible verses like 1 Corinthians 9:27 in its favour. Wrestling demanded a strict diet, which Jim followed for that reason and also because frugality in eating was a good help to spiritual discipline.

His letters from that period quoted by Elisabeth Elliot in *Shadow of the Almighty* are full of a deep longing and determination to know God better, and much evidence of spiritual discipline, which he also recommended to others. Writing to his sister Jane he advised:

> Begin each day with private reading of the Word and prayer. Bunyan has well said, 'Sin will keep you from this book, or this book will keep you from sin.' From the very first, as you begin high school, give out gospel tracts to those you meet. Make a bold start – it's easier that way, rather than trying to begin half-way through ...[3]

By the end of his first year at Wheaton he felt that spiritually it had been 'a profitable year', and his letters home were full of appreciation for his family and of the discoveries he was making every day about God, the truths of Scripture and the spiritual life. Yet the letters do not have the note of somebody surprised at discovering unsuspected truth, rather the pleasure of somebody finding that deeply-felt truths were being confirmed in daily experience in scores of ways.

He returned to Wheaton for his second, 'sophomore' year, somewhat disillusioned by the pursuit of academic knowledge: 'What thing better can a man know than the love of Christ, which passes knowledge?' He was particularly sceptical about studying philosophy, which he appears to have considered a rather pointless, arid speculation.

He comes across in his letters as undeniably rather 'pious', but the letters are probably misleading in that they communicate chiefly those things which Jim wanted to share with his family as he learned more and more about God and the Scriptures. His daily life, the rough and tumble of college, his relaxed relationships with fellow-students who thought of him as single-minded and 'especially "spiritual"', are aspects of his Wheaton days which do not figure largely in his letters home.

He was, for example, interested in football (though he felt that the cheering crowds would be better employed in shouting God's praises). He was invited to become business manager of the team, which would have brought with it great advantages, not least financial. He turned down the offer, though his family would have liked him to have accepted it. His father, too, was anxious for Jim to have as full an education as possible and to enjoy the opportunities that he himself had never had. Jim, however, was increasingly sceptical about 'knowledge': 'Education is dangerous, and, personally, I am beginning to question its value in a Christian life.'

He was becoming a successful sportsman, his wrestling skill earning him the nickname 'India-rubber Man'. He prayed before each bout, and he discovered that the physical exercise had good

results in his spiritual devotions and Bible study,
though his mother was alarmed by his wrestling
and would have preferred him to give it up. His
father had different concerns which had to be
soothed:

> My grades came through this week, and were, as
> expected, lower than last semester. However, I make
> no apologies, and admit I've let them drag a bit for
> study of the Bible, in which I seek the degree A.U.G.,
> 'Approved Unto God'.

JIM Elliot did not regard his first two years at college
as preparation for any specific Christian service: he
was determined to equip himself spiritually and
prepare himself physically for whatever God might
indicate he should do with his life. But at some time
during those twenty-four months – the exact time or
occasion is not known – he developed a passionate
concern for the Great Commission of Jesus, that his
followers should go and preach the gospel. Jim's
college notebook survives, and among hundreds of
names of people for whom he prayed regularly are
pages of statistics noted down in college: statistics
that demonstrate the immensity and urgency of the
missionary task.

In the summer vacation of 1947 he hitchhiked to
Mexico with a friend whose parents were missionaries in that country. He spent six weeks with the
family, weeks which became almost a mini-course

in mission strategy. Towards the end of his stay, having spent a month learning Spanish for the first time, he was invited to preach to local children. He decided to do it without an interpreter, and managed, to his great delight, to complete the assignment.

When the time came for him to leave Mexico, Jim Elliot knew what his life's calling was. He was determined to take God's word to those who had never heard it, though he still did not know the exact place and people: though he was sure that it would be somewhere in Latin America.

HE returned to Wheaton to commence his 'junior' (third) year of studies. He had not taken it for granted that he would be coming back: American college courses are usually four years, but Jim had thought he might only be able to afford to study for two. But the money was made available, and he came back to college having decided to take Greek as his major: besides the obvious advantages in biblical studies, he calculated that studying Greek would be a help in future language studies when he began his missionary training. His professors remember him as an enthusiastic, if not always entirely accurate, translator of the Greek classics, and he was very moved at being able to read the New Testament in its original language.[4]

He had by now acquired the label of somebody

not much interested in girls, though his good looks
and sporting ability would have guaranteed him a
busy social diary. Girl friends were just one of the
things he had come to regard as distractions in his
pursuit of God's plan for his life. But in his Greek
classes he met Elisabeth (Betty) Howard, sister of
Dave who was a member of the wrestling team, and
the two found themselves drawn to each other. Jim
accepted an invitation from Dave to spend Christmas with the family mainly because he wanted the
opportunity to see more of Elisabeth, of whom he
realised he was growing very fond. Their courtship
was quite untypical of student romances. They only
had one date together (they went to a missionary
meeting), and many hours studying together and
talking; but before long they were speaking openly
of their feelings for each other. Both acknowledged
the priority of God's plan for their lives, and they
prayed and struggled for months over whether God
had brought them together for marriage.

Jim had other struggles, too. By now he was
seeking God's guidance as to what form and direction his missionary work should take. He prayed
long and hard during his third year at Wheaton. The
following summer he joined three other students as
a team of the Foreign Missions Fellowship, part of
the Inter-Varsity Christian Fellowship, touring college campuses to encourage missionary awareness
among students.

It was a momentous time for Jim, who found

himself preaching with a new passion and with profound results: years later, young men and women entering the mission field were to point to his preaching on that tour as marking the point of their decision to dedicate their lives to missionary work. For Jim, his vision was still not entirely clear: writing to his brother Bert he mentioned that his interest in working among Latin-American peoples was mixed with an interest in work among North American Indians.

His study timetable for his final, 'senior' year included eight hours of Greek, some Hebrew, and textual criticism. He wrote to his parents saying how much his summer experiences had confirmed to him the need for Jesus to be at the absolute centre of the whole of his life. He wrote to them again some time later, telling them for the first time about his growing love for Elisabeth. The previous year, he told them, they had both decided that God wanted them to remain single for life. But now ... 'She leaves on Tuesday,' he told them wryly, 'for which I'm thankful, as I must think clearly if I'm to understand Hebrew and Greek.' When she left Wheaton, the couple began to write to each other, clearly expressing their mutual feelings and wondering what God had in store for them. Characteristically, Jim suggested that their letters to each other should not be frequent, as this would be a good discipline. 'We best learn patience by practising it,' he observed.

Jim and Elisabeth's courtship has much in common with that of an earlier missionary couple: C. T. Studd and Priscilla Stewart. Both couples were overwhelmingly anxious that their relationship should not displace the love that both partners had for Jesus: C. T. Studd's 'prescription' for Priscilla to sing daily –

> Jesus I love thee,
> Thou art to me
> Dearer than ever
> Charlie can be! –[5]

could have been written by Jim Elliot. Both men, too, in their anxiety to demonstrate that physical beauty would not distract them from their love of the Lord and desire to do his will, gave rather unflattering descriptions of their proposed fiancées in letters to family and friends! But Jim's journals, which he had begun the previous year, tell a moving story of increasing love for Elisabeth, a deep sense of loneliness without her, and an anguished determination to deny himself even this relationship if it were not totally within God's will for him and for Elisabeth. The journals frequently use the image of becoming a 'eunuch' for Christ's sake, and the quality of Jim's love for Elisabeth can be gauged by the scale of the sacrifice which he considered losing her would be.

He celebrated his twenty-first birthday on 8 October, overshadowed by the possibility of being drafted for National Service and by his frustration at not yet being out on the mission field: so many generations were perishing, he wrote to his parents, without hearing of the Saviour! Two days later, he wrote in his journal words that show that his goal had remained fixed since he became a student: 'Singleness, simplicity is required of me. One treasure, a single eye, and a sole master.'[6] He was able to write to his father not long afterwards,

> As regards Bets, I would have it no other way. God has made me eager to go singly to the work as I ever was. It would be fine with me – and I say this as praising His over-abounding grace – if I never saw her again ... I have no clear leading as to what work I am to be doing, so that a wife simply cannot be decided upon.[7]

November found him still unsure where his missionary calling would take him; he wrote to his family that he had a 'pervading concern' for work with Moslems, particularly in India. In the same letter, he made it clear that though he was at peace over the possibility of not marrying Elisabeth, his feelings for her remained strong.

By now president of the Foreign Missions Fellowship at Wheaton, Jim was struggling with a large

workload of academic studies, Christian service
and wrestling. He relished the challenge, though
there were frustrations: divisions in the student
Christian community, complacency in local and
national Christian movements with which he was
involved, and a troubling feeling of being unpro-
ductive and wasting time. In one mood of depression he wrote,

> Look at my days – how short they are, how unpro-
> ductive, how full of incidentals, how little real pro-
> duction for the Harvest-Master.[8]

December continued the frustration ('I think Solo-
mon remarks somewhere that "hope deferred
maketh the heart sick".'), but he was able to write
to his family that though he tended to be explicit
about his frustrations, he was happy. To Elisabeth
he wrote,

> I charge thee, Beloved, seek *His* counsel. The next
> year will be a crisis year for us both and we must
> individually find His path.[9]

The revelation of God's purpose came, in the end,
relatively quietly. At the close of the year Jim
attended the International Student Missionary Convention at Illinois University. There, as he wrote to
Elisabeth,

> The Lord has done what I wanted Him to do for me
> this week. I wanted primarily a peace about going

into pioneer Indian work. As I analyze my feelings now, I am quite at ease about saying that tribal work in the South American jungle is the general direction of my missionary purpose. Also, I am confident that God wants me to begin the jungle work single ...[10]

The final months of Jim Elliot's Wheaton years saw a number of changes. The quiet discovery of his 'general direction' seems to have been a release for him in several ways. He realised that many of his attitudes had been super-spiritual – 'priggish', he called them; worse, he had judged others by his own demanding standards and had thereby cut himself off from some parts of the student body whom he would have liked to have got to know. His letters became more relaxed, and he allowed himself to join in more of the fun of student life, though he confessed that he allowed the pendulum to swing too far and found his dependence on prayer and Bible study slipping; a situation he quickly corrected.

His early scepticism about 'knowledge', and his comment as a sophomore to his father, that he regarded academic grades as relatively unimportant by comparison with gaining God's approval, did not make him a failure as a student. On the contrary, he graduated with the highest honours.

THE story which was to become known throughout the world had only just begun. The narrowing of the 'general direction' to Ecuador, first with Peter

Fleming in 1951; the work with Indian tribes, leading inexorably to the strange Auca people, 'stone-age' Indians living in the jungle; the marriage of Jim and Elisabeth on Jim's twenty-sixth birthday; the arrival of others in Ecuador to join in the work, including Nate Saint, Roger Youderain and Ed McCully; and the tragedy on the Curary in which all five were killed just two weeks after Jim had greeted the Aucas face to face for the first time – these are described in other books by those who know the story intimately.

For many, the years described in this chapter are a very small part of the story of Jim Elliot, a necessary academic prelude to a missionary vocation that was concentrated for a few brief years in South America. But the most cursory glance at the letters and journals of the Wheaton years show that Jim regarded them as crucial years of preparation, as integral to his later work as any of the field experience and specific training that came later.

Yet he did not regard the single-mindedness and discipline of his student years as training for work with the Aucas, or even, at the beginning, for missionary work in general. So far as he knew when he entered Wheaton in 1945, God might have wanted him to be an executive in a New York office (it's fascinating to speculate what his witness might have been like in such a situation). He was convinced that to be a soldier in God's army, to be equipped for *any* service, it was necessary to cast aside everything that might hinder him, just as the writer to the Hebrews urges his readers:

> Therefore, since we are surrounded by such a great cloud of witnesses, let us throw off everything that hinders and the sin that so easily entangles, and let us run with perseverance the race marked out for us. (Hebrews 12:1)

It was not, for Jim, specialist training at all. He had no idea in high school or at Wheaton that he would in a few short years become one of the century's most publicised missionaries; or that he would be called to lay down his life in God's service, though he often contemplated the possibility. For Jim Elliot discipline and spiritual concentration, a ruthless casting off of all that might distract him from God's purposes, and an unswerving determination to know God better, were not part of any college syllabus or mission agenda. They were, quite simply, the marks of the normal Christian life.

ONE aspect of the Auca tragedy that astonished the world was what happened afterwards. Within a matter of months, four of the five widows were back in South America, continuing the work their husbands had begun. Nate Saint's sister Rachel continued to study the Auca language, and the Missionary Aviation Fellowship, whose pilot Nate had been, continued to drop gifts to the Aucas, some of whose homes were decorated with fabric torn from the plane that the team had landed in (and which, as I write, has only recently been recovered from the river). Later, Jim's widow Elisabeth and daughter Valerie joined Rachel, living and working among the Aucas. 'The goal of the five martyrs,' comments Russell Hitt, 'had been accomplished by two women and a tiny girl.'[11] In 1967 Rachel Saint attended the Berlin Congress on Evangelism, a groundbreaking initiative in many ways. She brought with her two Auca Indians.[12]

Today, nearly all the jungle tribes in Ecuador have churches and the Bible in their own languages, often through the work of missionary societies with whom Jim and his colleagues were associated: the Brethren, the Missionary Aviation Fellowship, the Summer Institute of Linguistics, Wycliffe Bible Translators, the Gospel Missionary Union and others.[13]

Notes

1. The information for much of this chapter comes from the writings of Elisabeth Elliot. Quotations without references are taken from her biography of her husband, *Shadow of the Almighty* (1958: currently O. M. Publishing, 1988). I am also grateful to the staff of the Archives and Special Collections Dept., Wheaton College, for providing me with information and resources.

2. Today the restrictions have altered, and in the current college prospectus, prospective students are told, for example, of the cultural resources of Chicago including the performing arts. This does not reflect an abandoning of a call to personal discipline and Christian lifestyle, however, as can be seen for example in the

academically impressive approach to media and communications studies, where students are taught to scrutinise such areas in the light of Scripture.

3. Quoted in *Shadow of the Almighty*, p.40.

4. Elisabeth Elliot, *Through Gates of Splendour*, p.17.

5. Norman P. Grubb, *C. T. Studd: Cricketer and Pioneer* (Religious Tract Society, 1933), p. 87.

6. Elisabeth Elliot, ed., *The Journals of Jim Elliot* (USA: Fleming H. Revell, 1978), p.93.

7. Quoted in *Shadow of the Almighty*, p.87.

8. Ibid, p.96.

9. Ibid, p.106.

10. Ibid, p.109.

11. Russell T. Hitt, *Jungle Pilot: the Life and Witness of Nate Saint* (Hodder & Stoughton, 1960), p.301.

12. David Porter, *Arts and Minds* (Hodder and Stoughton, 1993), p.87-88.

13. Statistics and other information available in Patrick Johnstone, *Operation World* (O. M. Publishing, 5th edn 1993), pp. 201-203.

8

C. S. Lewis
Surprise – and Joy

Of all the people included in the present book, Lewis is the only one who has an international cult following today. The C. S. Lewis industry is large. Over thirty years after his death, almost all the books he wrote are still in print; his novels for adults and children remain widely read, and some have been filmed several times; and numerous conferences, academic courses and other functions both local and international attract thousands of interested Lewis fans. In recent years the story of Lewis's marriage to Joy Davidman has had a wide audience, first as the television play *Shadowlands*, then as the stage play and film of the same name. The irony is that Lewis would probably have deplored it all. Though he was a professor, broadcaster and public speaker, he was a somewhat private person who married late, was sometimes clumsy and uneasy with students and preferred a circle of close, mainly male, literary friends to a broad social life.

Yet it might be said that for many Lewis is the closest we have had to a Protestant evangelical saint, certainly insofar as his memory is revered. The picture of the Oxbridge professor with a silver tongue and gifted pen, who made Christianity understandable to the man and woman in the street, whose personality was bluff and manly and whose personal spirituality enabled him to overcome deep tragedy, is an attractive one. So much is Lewis – who was an essentially kindly and modest man – regarded as a modern hero of the faith, that other views are often regarded by his devotees as heresy. But idolatry does nobody any service, and often a better idea is gained of the way God uses his most strategic men and women if we ignore the myths that others build round them; myths which, in Lewis's case, he would have disowned even if he had recognised them.

CLIVE Staples Lewis was born in 1898 in Belfast. His father was a solicitor. His early memories were of family holidays, of playing with his older brother Warren ('Warnie') Lewis, and of the rambling suburban house, Little Lea, to which the family moved in 1905. The mysterious attic spaces and views across the mountains were to reappear years later in the Narnia stories for children.

Soon after the move, Warnie was sent to boarding school in England, and Lewis (who was 'Jack' to his friends all his life) was taught at home by a governess. He read voraciously from the books that filled the house (though he later lamented that his parents' choice of books was very different to the

kind of books he preferred as he grew older), and
wrote his earliest stories – about Animal-Land, a
fantasy country. So he passed the time, between
Warnie's holidays.

When Jack was nine his childhood world disin-
tegrated. After a brief struggle with cancer, his
mother died. 'With my mother's death all settled
happiness, all that was tranquil and reliable, disappeared from my life,' he wrote later[1]. Jack's father
never recovered from the shock of bereavement,
and as the years went by the relationship between
him and Jack grew more and more strained.

Shortly afterwards he was sent to join Warnie at
boarding school in England. The regime was harsh
and the education minimal; a year later, the school
closed down and Jack went on to a prep school at
Malvern. It was there that he discovered Norse
mythology, which was to become an obsession.

> Pure 'Northernness' engulfed me: a vision of huge,
> clear spaces hanging above the Atlantic in the end-
> less twilight of Northern summer, remoteness, se-
> verity ...[2]

At fourteen, Jack gained a scholarship to Malvern
College; Warnie was now studying with a tutor,
preparing for admission to the Royal Military Academy at Sandhurst. Despite broadening his reading
during many enjoyable hours in the school library,
Jack hated Malvern with its enclosed rituals and
stratified school hierarchy. After a year he pleaded

successfully with his father to be allowed to leave.

One of Malvern's few positive aspects for Jack had been his form master Harry Wakelyn Smith, who first introduced him to the joys of poetry. Another cherished guide and mentor, to whom he would always be grateful, now entered his life; W. T. Kirkpatrick – the 'Great Knock', as the Lewises called him – who had tutored Warnie (now successfully installed at Sandhurst) and who now agreed to tutor Jack. At the same time, Jack met Arthur Greeves, a neighbour's son. The two shared a deep enthusiasm for all things Norse; a friendship was struck that was to continue for the rest of Jack's life.

1914 saw the outbreak of war and the beginning of Jack's studies with Kirkpatrick, with whom he studied for almost three years and through whom he discovered a huge range of new authors. Warnie went to fight in France. The years with Kirkpatrick were among the happiest Jack ever spent.

THROUGH books, Jack's spiritual boundaries had been repeatedly extended; the Northernness of the Viking romances, magical worlds of Old English romance, tales of chivalry and heroism, and a little book by Scottish minister George MacDonald called *Phantastes*, all awoke spiritual resonances in the young student. In later life he was responsible for introducing George MacDonald to a contemporary readership[3], but at that time he was not much interested in formal religion. Confirmed in 1914 to please his father, he confided to Arthur Greeves that he considered religion to be a purely human invention; though he also described his discovery of Phantastes to Arthur as the 'baptising' of his imagination.

In 1917, encouraged by Kirkpatrick, Jack became an Oxford student. His performance in the entrance examination was not brilliant, but Oxford was a way into the army and a commission. He went to France later that year and saw action at the Front; but in 1918 he was wounded by shrapnel and was invalided home.

He took a Triple First from Oxford in 1923, obtained a temporary lectureship in philosophy at his old college, University College, and then was appointed a Fellow of Magdalen College. He taught at Oxford until 1954, when he was appointed to the newly established Chair of Mediaeval and Renaissance literature at Cambridge.

AMONG his pupils were critics as different as Kenneth Tynan and Harry Blamires, and poets as different as John Wain and John Betjeman; among his friends were the scholar and storyteller J. R. R. Tolkien, the novelist, dramatist, critic and poet Charles Williams, the scholar Neville Coghill, the lawyer and writer Owen Barfield and Jack's brother Warnie. These and several others were members of a group of friends called the Inklings who met 'to drink Beer and to discuss, among other things, the books they were writing'[4]. It was to this circle that such books as Tolkien's *The Lord of the Rings*, Charles Williams' Arthurian poems and many of Lewis's works were first read aloud.

Warnie made his home with Jack in 1931; they lived at The Kilns, a house which they shared with an older woman, Mrs Janie Moore – 'Minto'. During the war Jack had fought in France alongside her son Paddy, and had promised him that if Paddy died he would look after Minto. Paddy Moore was killed in action; Lewis shouldered the responsibility he had promised, and gave money and other support to his mother and her young daughter, secretly at first while he was still an undergraduate. The Kilns was jointly purchased by Jack, Warnie and Minto, and Jack continued to devote himself to her needs until she died in 1951.

It is a measure of the strength of the 'Lewis cult' that when A. N. Wilson made the reasonable suggestion that there may have been some physical relationship between Jack and Minto, many of C. S. Lewis's admirers were outraged; and certainly there is no hint of it in Lewis's writings. Yet, as Wilson points out, it was by no means unthinkable. When they met, Jack was a young man of twenty; Minto, who was separated from her husband, was a pretty forty-five year old:

Neither of them was a Christian believer, nor were they bound by any code of morality which would have forbidden them to become lovers in the fullest sense of the word.[5]

Warnie disliked Minto, and many of Jack's friends could not understand why he had committed himself to look after her, especially as she grew older and displayed mood swings and periods of irrationality; the relationship had by then long settled into a dull tedium. When younger she made such demands on Jack's time that his work suffered.

He was a fluent and rapid prose writer. But his first major prose work – *The Allegory of Love* – took about eight years to complete. This was the price he paid for having thrown in his lot with a person who with all her virtues – generosity, warmth of character, genuine and passionate admiration, as well as love, for Lewis himself – did not have the concept of a working day. She belonged to that great majority of intelligent human beings who think of a book as something with which to beguile the hours of solitude of an evening.[6]

As she 'entered her dotage', observes Wilson, Lewis's literary output increased dramatically.

But if Wilson is right in his suggestion that the relationship was a sexual one between two people who were not married to each other, one event during those years would change it completely: the conversion of C. S. Lewis to Christianity.

THE first seeds of Lewis's faith were sown by friends. Arthur Greeves was a devout Christian, and their correspondence had become so heated on the subject that the matter had been dropped by mutual agreement. At Oxford Jack met Owen Barfield, whose arguments against Jack's atheism the latter described as the 'Great War between us', Neville Coghill – 'a Christian and a thoroughgoing supernaturalist', and Hugo Dyson and J. R. R. Tolkien, both of whom were also Christians. 'And so the great Angler played the fish,' Jack recalled later, 'and I never dreamed the hook was in my tongue.'

> [Jack's] friendships, like many of the books he had been reading, were filled with traps for the unwary atheist. 'All over the board,' he was later to write, 'my pieces were in the most disadvantageous positions. Soon I could no longer cherish even the illusion that the initiative lay with me. My Adversary began to make his final moves.' [7]

Since childhood, Jack had been consumed by a longing for beauty, for 'joy', a desire fuelled by the serene vistas of Ireland and later the bleak, severe beauty of the Norse landscape. It was joy that satisfied him in the works of George MacDonald:

> The quality which had enchanted me in his imaginative works turned out to be the quality of the real universe, the divine, magical, terrifying and ecstatic reality in which we all live. [8]

Now he began to understand that something lay behind the joy which he had sought.

> In my scheme of thought it is not blasphemous to compare the error which I was making with that error which the angel in the Sepulchre rebuked when he said to the women, 'Why seek ye the living among the dead? He is not here, He is risen.' The comparison is of course between something of infinite moment and something very small; like comparison between the Sun and the Sun's reflection in a dewdrop.[9]

Step by step, assisted by many influences and several friends (in *Surprised by Joy* Jack describes both influences and friends in some detail), he moved from his youthful agnosticism and his later romantic yearning for joy, to a position which demanded an acceptance that God not only existed but was making just demands upon him:

> You must picture me alone in that room at Magdalen, night after night, feeling, whenever my mind lifted even for a second from my work, the steady, unrelenting approach of Him whom I so earnestly desired not to meet. In the Trinity Term of 1929 I gave in, and admitted that God was God, and knelt and prayed: perhaps, that night, the most dejected and reluctant convert in all England.[10]

'It must be understood,' Jack acknowledged, 'that the conversion recorded in the last chapter was only to Theism.' He began to attend church, but it was 'merely a symbolical and provisional practice'. It would not be until two years later that, with the help of Hugo Dyson and J. R. R. Tolkien, he would take the second and final step, from Theism to Christianity. Typically, his journey involved a good deal of intellectual discussion and theological argument. There is something of a divine irony in the fact that his final surrender was not an intellectual encounter at all.

> I know very well when, but hardly how, the final step was taken. I was driven to Whipsnade one sunny morning. When we set out I did not believe that Jesus Christ is the Son of God, and when we reached the zoo I did. Yet I had not exactly spent the journey in thought. Nor in great emotion. 'Emotional' is perhaps the last word we can apply to some of the most important events. It was more like when a man, after long sleep, still lying motionless in bed, becomes aware that he is awake ...[11]

Jack and Minto's physical relationship, if it existed, now ceased; Jack's new-found faith brought with it a moral conviction and a determination to live out practically what he had accepted spiritually. But of course, much else had changed as well.

JACK had shown early talent as a writer, his childhood fables about Animal-Land being only a beginning. His early poetry, published as *Spirits in Bond-*

age: a Cycle of Lyrics (1919) and *Dymer* (1926), was written under the pseudonym 'Clive Hamilton'. Both books were admired and the latter won extravagant praise from the critic Arthur Quiller-Couch. Jack was far from being a Christian, but the poetry contains seeds of his later writings. He continued to write poems all his life, and some were included in later collections of his verse.

In 1933 Jack published his first prose work, *The Pilgrim's Regress*. It was also his first publication as a Christian. He later considered it an over-intellectual, unsatisfactory book, though it is an interesting reflection of its times and does present well Jack's fascination with the theme of joy. It was also partly a working-out of some themes he was exploring in his Oxford lectures, to be published in 1936 as *The Allegory of Love*. The 1936 work made his name as a scholar. Colin Duriez's assessment that the book – on the mediaeval traditions of allegory and courtly love – is 'among the outstanding works of literary criticism of the century'[12] is confirmed not only by noted scholars such as J. A. W. Bennett but also by students ever since.

Many of the Oxford lectures found their way into print only later: *The Discarded Image* (1964) was based on two early lecture series, 'Prolegomena to Mediaeval Studies' and 'Prolegomena to Renaissance Studies'. The word means 'preliminary discussion' and few students ever received so illuminating a preface to their reading of a literary period.

In the early 1940s Jack was, in Dame Helen Gardner's words,

> ... by far the most impressive and exciting person in the Faculty of English. He had behind him a major work of literary history; he filled the largest lecture-room available for his lectures; and the Socratic Club, which he founded and over which he presided, for the free discussion of religious and philosophic questions, was the most flourishing and influential of undergraduate societies.[13]

In 1942 he published an influential defence of Milton's poetry, *A Preface to Paradise Lost*. It was a combative work, arguing against the position of F. R. Leavis and the 'Scrutiny' school of critics who, Jack argued, far from illuminating Milton's great poem actually prevented a proper reading of it. A book published a few years earlier, *The Personal Heresy* (1939), was also polemical; it was the record of a controversy between Jack and E. M. W. Tillyard, with whose interpretation of *Paradise Lost* he had disagreed. Jack argued that poetry was not, and should not be, the expression of the poet's personality; Tillyard challenged Jack's 'objective' or 'impersonal' theory of poetry.

ALTHOUGH by the time of the publication of the *Preface* in 1942 Jack had made his mark on Oxford as a scholar, English literature was not the only subject on which he had published books. *The*

Problem of Pain (1940) was the first of several
works of Christian apologetics, including *Miracles*
(1947); they were marked by intellectual brilliance,
learning, and a powerful use of argument. Besides
these he wrote much more popular books, including
the phenomenally successful *The Screwtape Letters*
(1942), letters from a senior to a junior devil entrusted
with the oversight of a young man destined for
damnation; unfortunately, his charge becomes a Christian. The book (which cost Jack much emotional
and spiritual energy and depressed him constantly)
was in a long tradition of literary irony and fantasies
about supernatural beings, but it caught the imagination of the public and was instantly successful.

Those who discovered C. S. Lewis through
Screwtape did not have to enter the world of literary
criticism or theological debate to enjoy his work
further and consider his powerful and winsome
arguments for Christianity. There were, for example, several books of the texts of broadcast talks on
central Christian themes given by Jack beginning
early in 1941. Their clarity, directness, and lack of
academic pretentiousness appealed to thousands of
listeners, though Jack was not an ideal broadcaster
(he tended to bellow at the microphone, and his use
of public school slang irritated George Orwell, for
one, intensely). Later the talks were revised and
republished as *Mere Christianity* (1952), probably
Jack's best-known work of non-fiction and one that
was immensely influential.

Mere Christianity is, for many Christians, not nearly specific enough. Jack's Arminianism shows clearly in his discussion of free will, and many Reformed and Calvinist critics regard this as an almost fatal weakness. More generally seen as a weakness is the end of the book, where Jack leaves the reader with the picture of being in a large entrance hall with many rooms leading off it; the reader may now choose which brand of Christianity he prefers and which denominational and doctrinal package he will opt for.

But Lewis was clear about the purpose of the talks and the books that came from them. He was interested in pre-evangelism, rather than evangelism; he wanted, as it were, to arouse in his listeners and readers that same awareness of an infinite and moral God that had been part of his own life since childhood, and towards whose source his own pilgrimage had been so protracted and often painful. The discussions about churchmanship and Christian variations could come later. Jack's aim was to persuade people to face up to the fact that they were real persons, living in a moral universe, created by a personal God who had a claim on the men, women and children he had created.

In 1938 Jack had published *Out of the Silent Planet*, the first of a science fiction trilogy that was completed by *Perelandra* (1943) and *That Hideous Strength* (1945). It is an uneven trio; the finest is certainly the second novel (later renamed *Voyage to Venus*), though the first novel is a competent and exciting tale in the tradition of H. G. Wells, whom Jack admired. The final novel, however, is burdened by a complicated plot and a confusing collection of themes. The trilogy tells the story of Ransome, who is abducted to Mars by two scientists who think that its ruler demands human sacrifice.

The trilogy works out the themes of unfallen beings and their reaction to fallen Earth the 'silent planet'; the strange ruler of Deep Heaven, Maleldil, and the Oyarsa his servants; and the gross offence to the courtesy of Deep Heaven that Earth represents. In the second volume Ransome is called to Perelandra (Venus) to fight Weston, one of his captors from the earlier volume and now consecrated to evil. In a deeply symbolic struggle with this 'un-man', Ransome is wounded and learns the theological significance of his own name. In the final volume the action moves to Earth, where a nightmare scientific utopia challenges and corrupts the essential goodness that illuminates Perelandra. Woven into the complex story are the themes of Merlin the enchanter and Ransome himself, now seen to be the great Pendragon of Logres.

The first two volumes were well received by science fiction enthusiasts, and the trilogy has remained in print since it was first published. Far more accessible, however, and of a quite different order of inspiration, are Jack's masterly stories for children about the mysterious world of Narnia.

Beginning with *The Lion, the Witch and the Wardrobe* (1950), seven stories tell the history of the land of Narnia from its creation to its final consummation in *The Last Battle* (1956). Although in the first volume there is a moving parable of the death and resurrection of Jesus, and he is richly and powerfully portrayed in the figure of Aslan the lion who dominates all seven books, it is quite possible to enjoy all seven books without ever realising that they are an allegory of the Christian faith. Yet it is also impossible to read them without realising that the world of Narnia is driven by something that stands beyond and above the reason and control of human beings; what Jack called the Deep Magic, that existed before Narnia began.

Generations of children have enjoyed the books, as have countless adults. The Narnia stories are admittedly now old-fashioned (but so are E. N. Nesbit's books and those of many other popular children's writers); and Jack is prone to be rather 'adult' and arch in some of his authorial asides. Yet the books (which have been performed on stage, have been turned into board games and comics, and have also been televised both as cartoons and feature films) have influenced many children towards Christianity, and those who read them with care will find the whole Christian gospel spelt out in their pages.

'It means,' said Aslan, 'that though the Witch knew the Deep Magic, there is a magic deeper still which

she did not know. Her knowledge goes back only to
the dawn of time. But if she could have looked a little
further back, into the stillness and darkness before
Time dawned, she would have read there a different
incantation. She would have known that when a
willing victim who had committed no treachery was
killed in a traitor's stead, the Table would crack and
Death itself would start working backwards.[14]

The Narnia stories extended Jack's already international readership. Among his readers was an American, Joy Gresham. Joy was a writer; she and her
husband Bill had both published novels; Bill's first,
Nightmare Alley, had earned enough money to give
them a comfortable lifestyle. Joy was Jewish, and
both of them had been Marxists, but they had been
converted to Christianity partly by reading Jack's
books. Joy began to write to him, discussing points
in the books and asking him questions about Christianity.

The Greshams had two sons, a comfortable
home and a difficult marriage. Bill's attachment to
Christianity turned out to be temporary, and in
September 1952, ostensibly in connection with her
writing projects and family obligations but mainly
to give her an opportunity to reflect about her
deteriorating marriage, Joy went to England. High
on her list of priorities was to meet Jack, who was
by now her chief spiritual advisor even though they
had not met. It was a difficult time for Jack, too. His
life had changed dramatically the previous year

with the death of Minto, and his own 'spiritual director' Walter Adams had died in May 1952.

Joy made her base in London. Travelling to Oxford she met Lewis, who found her delightful. He invited her to spend Christmas at The Kilns; she spent a fortnight there. During that time she showed Jack a letter from Bill informing her that he was in love with another woman and considered the marriage to be at an end.

Jack was fifty-four, Joy thirty-seven years old. He was busy with his monumental *English Literature in the Sixteenth Century (excluding Drama)*, commissioned for the Oxford History of English Literature and published in 1954. Joy, back in America, yielded to Bill's demands for a divorce, and decided to make a new home for herself in England with her sons. Jack helped her with the various problems she encountered, not least when he found her, and paid for, a home in Oxford. He himself was now commuting to his new duties as Cambridge Professor of English Mediaeval and Renaissance Literature; Joy was beginning a new career as a writer, under her maiden name of Joy Davidman.

The friendship deepened, but both held strong views on the sanctity of Christian marriage and the undesirability of divorce and re-marriage. Yet in April 1956, Jack and Joy were married. A civil marriage in a registry office, Jack considered, was not a marriage in the Christian sense, and this was wholly a marriage of convenience, Jack's ultimate act of help to Joy; there was no other way that she and her sons could obtain residency rights in Britain.

Although from Jack's point of view the marriage was in name only (though close friends saw even then that Jack was already falling in love with her), Joy's circumstances made it necessary for her to leave her own home and move with her sons to The Kilns. It was there that an accident led to the discovery that Joy was suffering from inoperable cancer. Jack, distraught both by Joy's illness and the parallels with his own childhood (Joy's sons were much the same age as he had been when his own mother had died of cancer), realised at last that he had fallen in love with Joy. On 21 March 1957, Jack and Joy were married in a hospital ward, and later Joy came back to The Kilns to spend what everybody thought would be her final days with Jack.

Matters turned out miraculously different. Prayers for healing were followed by a remission that lasted for two years, during which Joy transformed the bachelor establishment at The Kilns (neither she nor Jack would hear of Warnie leaving), and Jack's relationship with Joy's sons grew stronger. But the remission was short-lived, and by March 1960 the cancer was back, now rampant and uncontrollable. A last holiday together was spent in Greece, which they had longed to visit, but on their return Joy's condition worsened rapidly. She died on 13 July, 1960.

THE slow and agonising progress through grief, the near-loss of faith, the doubt and anger against God are chronicled both by Jack's friends (whose accounts form much of the basis for the book, play and films of *Shadowlands*) and by Jack himself, notably in *A Grief Observed* (1961). A complementary, practical exposition of the theoretical discussions of the earlier *The Problem of Pain*, the book was published under a pseudonym 'N. W. Clerk' and chronicles Jack's feelings for Joy and his road back to faith after the grief of her death.

His final years were marked by an abiding sense of loss, and concern over Warnie's life-long struggle with alcoholism. There were more books: *Letters to Malcolm: Chiefly on Prayer* (published posthumously in 1964) affirmed his confidence in heaven, but perhaps the most poignant of his thoughts are to be found in the letters he wrote while very ill in the last few months of his life. In a letter to a friend in September 1963 he wrote,

> I was unexpectedly revived from a long coma, and perhaps the almost continuous prayers of my friends did it – but it wd. have been a luxuriously easy passage, and one almost regrets having the door shut in one's face. Ought one to honour Lazarus rather than Stephen as the protomartyr? To be brought back and have all one's dying to do again was rather hard.

> When you die, and if 'prison visiting' is allowed, come down and look me up in Purgatory.

> It is all rather fun – solemn fun – isn't it?[15]

The letter encapsulates several aspects of C. S. Lewis. The gentle academic allusion, the total dependence on the grace and goodness of God, the insistence that Christianity is not humbug or tedium but is simply the most real, wholesome and enjoyable life possible for human beings; and the reference to Purgatory, which ought to remind us that despite the fact that many Christian groups including evangelicals have claimed him as their champion, he often defied comfortable theological categories and fits into no stereotype or cult.

He died on the same day (22 November 1963) as John F. Kennedy and Aldous Huxley, a juxtaposition which would probably have amused him. A measure of his influence is that unlike many people who are popular when alive, his reputation did not diminish after his death and there was no period of neglect. His ministry today is more extensive than ever. No doubt he would have put up with the attention and the embarrassment for the sake of the further spreading of the truth for which he fought so hard, rigorously and brilliantly.

Notes

1. C. S. Lewis, *Surprised by Joy* (1955: Collins Fontana edn, 1959), p 23.
2. *Ibid*, p 62.
3. Principally in his introduction and selections in C. S. Lewis (ed), *George MacDonald: an Anthology* (Geoffrey Bles, 1946).
4. From a plaque in the Eagle and Child public house, St Giles, Oxford, where the Inklings met 'every Tuesday morning, be-

tween the years 1939-1962 in the back room of this their favourite pub'.

5. A. N. Wilson, *C. S. Lewis: a Biography* (Collins, 1990), p 54.

6. *Ibid*, p 93.

7. Brian Sibley, *Shadowlands: the Story of C. S. Lewis and Joy Davidman* (Hodder & Stoughton, 1985), p 42.

8. C. S. Lewis (ed), *George MacDonald: an Anthology* (Geoffrey Bles, 1946), p 21.

9. C. S. Lewis, *Surprised by Joy*, p 135.

10. *Ibid*, p 182.

11. *Ibid*, p 189.

12. Colin Duriez, *The C. S. Lewis Handbook* (Monarch, 1990), p 16.

13. Helen Gardner, *Clive Staples Lewis 1898-1963*, Proc. British Academy, vol li (1965), p 424.

14. C. S. Lewis, *The Lion, the Witch and the Wardrobe* (1950: Puffin edn, 1959), p 148.

15. W. H. Lewis (ed), *Letters of C. S. Lewis* (Bles, 1966), p 307.

9

Francis Schaeffer
The Mountain Pastor

Huémoz-sur-Ollon is a picture-postcard mountain village nestling in the Swiss Alps, looking out over the town of Aigle and the Rhone Valley. High above, the jagged peaks of the Dents du Midi brood over the valley. In summer the fields are packed with flowers, drenching the slopes with colour beneath the mysterious dark woods that cloak the upper hillsides before giving way to the windswept peaks: in winter the snow comes further down the mountains and the fashionable slopes are thick with skiers. It is a region of peaceful solitude, even when the tourists come. At evening the cows amble down the slopes from pasture, their bells chiming in the still air, a sound that carries miles and seems to be made up of entire orchestras of instruments.

Huémoz is situated in the Canton of Vaud, in French-speaking Switzerland. It was in this area that the French Reformer Guillaume Farel, a colleague of John Calvin, lived and worked for a time during the European Reformation of the sixteenth century. In the nineteenth century revival movements originating in Germany swept the region and revitalised French Protestantism. In the twentieth century new and different religious movements made their mark on Switzerland, partly because several wealthy religious leaders made their base in neutral, prosperous Switzerland and partly because in the 1960s and 1970s it was a scenic route to the countries of the East.

And it was to this spot, tucked away on the beautiful mountainside, that an American family came in 1955, thrown out of neighbouring Champéry for having 'a religious influence', and now perplexed. Why had God, having called them to Europe as missionaries, chosen to take them away from a place where there had been plentiful opportunities to serve him, and put them in this mountain village where they would have to start all over again?

IT might seem strange that an American missionary organisation should think it necessary to send missionaries to Europe – to Calvin's country, no less, the historic heartland of the European Reformation. But the Independent Board for Presbyterian Foreign Missions had a burden for Europe, and Francis Schaeffer had played a large part in awakening that concern. In the summer of 1947 he had gone to Europe for the Board to 'survey the Christian situation as it exists in a number of places'. His reports to the Board and to the American Council of Christian Churches were a major factor in the convening of an international Reformed and evangelical conference in Holland in 1948 and the launch of a number of international evangelical initiatives.

Schaeffer argued that European Christian modernism, as seen for example in the work of theologians like Karl Barth and Reinhold Niebuhr, was actually a form of paganism. He found a loss of biblical foundations, in America as in England. He affirmed that Christianity was a revolutionary religion, and the modernists' blurring of theological distinctives and rejection of the notion of truth and error made them pagan.

> Let us not be deceived. These three forms of false religion which call themselves Christian [Roman Catholicism, Greek Orthodoxy and Modernistic Protestantism] are basically one and in their essence, they are pagan. They are together false religions .... We must not forget that those who are intertwined with these three forms of false religion, which bear the name of Christian, but are not, present to us as necessary a mission field as those who are enmeshed in black voodoo or in atheism.[1]

The battle for theological truth was not a new thing for Schaeffer, any more than heresy was a new discovery for him in Europe. Converted at the age of eighteen after reading the Bible (brought up in a nominally Christian home, attending a liberal Presbyterian church and seeking for a philosophy for life, he had felt it only fair to include the Bible in his search), he had been a brilliant college graduate and had gone on to theological seminary. He met his future wife Edith Seville at a church meeting where they both argued against the speaker's thesis that the Bible was not inspired and Jesus was not God's son. It is appropriate that they met as fellow fighters for God's truth; the battle for truth was to continue for the rest of their life together.

It was a time when bitter controversy was tearing the Presbyterian churches of North America apart. Schaeffer was enrolled in Westminster Theological Seminary, founded in 1929 by Gresham Machen and other leading Presbyterians to defend conservative protestant theology at the highest academic level. The Northern Presbyterian Church of which Schaeffer was a member was now headed by theological liberals. In 1936 matters came to a head when Machen was defrocked, dismissed from the ministry for his uncompromising adherence to a doctrine of verbal inspiration of Scripture and to the truths of the historic Christian faith.

Schaeffer saw the issue as a simple choice between alternatives. Those who defended the inspiration and authority of Scripture and evangelical Christianity had two options. Either they could remain in their denominations and bring the heretics to trial as followers of a false religion, or they could withdraw from their denominations and found new ones that would teach truth and speak against

Modernism. 'Normal separation,' he argued, 'was
neglected from 1900 to 1920 and so, like the
Protestant Reformation of four hundred years ago,
we are in a position of *separation in reverse. We* are
outside, instead of the heretic being outside; however, being outside by God's grace, and for His
glory, "Here we stand."'[2]

It was a period about which Schaeffer said little
in his prolific writings and lectures. Only after his
death, with the publication of the authorised *Letters*, is it now possible to gauge the depth of sorrow
that separation caused him, and his own awareness
that he had not been without fault. An illuminating
comment from a letter of 1951 shows something of
the spirit with which he was to fight for truth in the
years to come:

> Don't misunderstand me: from my experience here
> [in Europe] I am sure that we were correct in saying
> that the National Association of Evangelicals [against
> whom Schaeffer argued strongly in the theological
> conflicts of the 1930s] was wrong. But we could
> have remembered that, wrong though they were,
> they are for the most part brothers in Christ .... Now
> differences arise between us. Quickly the pattern
> repeats itself; the habit is too well learned. The
> movement is in jeopardy! So everything is thrown
> again .... And who is wounded? We are and our Lord
> .... I am sure 'separation' is correct, but it is only one
> principle. There are others to be kept as well. The
> command to love should mean something.[3]

It was a theme that ran through all his writings and teaching. In his critique of theological liberalism, *The Church Before the Watching World* (1971), he made a similarly poignant plea against separation without love:

> Don't divide into ugly parties. If you do, the world will see an ugliness which will turn it off. Your children will see the ugliness, and you will lose some of your sons and daughters .... Don't throw your children away, don't throw other people away by forgetting to observe, by God's grace, the two principles simultaneously – to show love and to practise the purity of the visible church.[4]

In 1936 Gresham Machen, forced by an irreducible point of principle, led a separation which resulted, after Machen's death in 1937, in the foundation of Faith Theological Seminary. Its first principal was Dr Allen MacRae, who had been assistant professor of Old Testament at Westminster Seminary and resigned over differences regarding secondary matters of biblical interpretation, particularly on eschatology.[5] Francis Schaeffer was a founder-member of the new seminary, and after graduating held a number of pastorates before going to Europe in 1947.

In the context of the unique ministry that was to occupy the rest of his life, it may seem that these years can only have been a mere waiting period. But Schaeffer emphasised throughout his life that he regarded himself primarily as a pastor and evangelist. The experience he gained, in churches in Grove City and Chester (both in Pennsylvania) and in St Louis Missouri, was a fundamental part of his training. It was important that the future leaders of what *Time* magazine (misleadingly) called 'a mission to intellectuals' should first minister to communities of widely varying backgrounds. There was a deeper value, too. It was in those years that Francis and Edith Schaeffer learned that though the uneducated person and the brilliant intellectual frame their questions very differently, they both have the same need of God and are seeking the same answers. Schaeffer's sermons attempted to present biblical truth in terms that were understandable to anybody, whoever they might be.

In 1948 the Schaeffers moved to Lausanne in Switzerland. They were to be mainly involved in Christian work with children, and they were also involved in the setting up of the International Council of Christian Churches, an initiative that owed a great deal to Schaeffer's reports from Europe the previous year. Francis also accepted speaking engagements in various parts of Europe, which he used as the opportunity to further challenge his hearers to confront the rise of Modernistic Liberalism and to take seriously the rising tide of existentialist thought that was appearing in some of the most influential theology. The following year they moved again, this time to the canton of Valais and the village of Champéry.

To devote so much space to this period of Schaeffer's life, when the work that made him famous had not yet started, may seem unnecessary. But it is not easy to understand the unique ministry of L'Abri without some awareness of the various strands that fed it: the background of denominational crisis that overshadowed Schaeffer's theological training, the pastoral gifts that matured over three pastorates, the battle for biblical truth that characterised Schaeffer's ministry from the earliest days, and the commitment to young people, who found in the Schaeffers a couple who were prepared to listen to their questions and acknowledge that questions demanded answers.

THE brief discussion of life in the Spirit in *True Spirituality* [6] was the product of a period early in 1951 when Francis Schaeffer went through a major spiritual crisis. Again, it is the *Letters* that show most clearly what was happening in his life at that time. He was forced to face the fact that while his fight for truth had been valid and necessary, and the bitter struggles in American Presbyterianism really had been about issues worth struggling for, there was a lack of reality in the spirituality of many of his fellow-combatants and certainly in his own. A turning-point was a conference at Easter 1951 at which Schaeffer spoke and where he heard the Scotsman Hugh Alexander speak.

While there, the Lord really spoke to my heart. I had
never heard anyone talk and sing about the combat
the way those people did. And yet at the same time
there was such a spiritual emphasis on the dependence of the leading of the Holy Spirit, identification
with Christ, the need of dying to serve the Lord, and
so on and so on, that since being there I felt the burden
lifted away. Not that I think the problem is less, but
for the first time I see the basic answer. It is the thing
for which I have been groping, I think. It is not less
combat, but a balance between it and a real following
of the leading of the Holy Spirit – in short, a care that
we do not minimize our personal spiritual lives.

I really feel lighter than I have for years .... God
willing, I do not want to lose this joy I have before the
Lord.[7]

It was the final piece of the jigsaw, the last stage in
God's preparation. Schaeffer emerged from the
crisis with a new emphasis on sanctification, a
renewed commitment to the truth of the Christian
faith, and a conviction that, while faith can never be
mathematically proven, there are *sufficient* reasons
given in the Bible for human beings to know that the
infinite, personal God really does exist and that
Christianity is true. And it is possible to embrace
that faith without committing intellectual suicide.

In 1953-54, the Schaeffers returned to America on
furlough. They now had four children – Priscilla,

Susan, Debby and Franky, who was two years old.
Schaeffer gave numerous addresses on the subject
of the deeper spiritual life and was also awarded an
honorary doctorate by Highland College, Long
Beach. It was a hectic furlough for Mrs Schaeffer
too, as she worked her way through a crowded
speaking programme.

It was hard to spare the time, though they were
looking forward to visiting America again. Much
had been happening in Champéry. Conversations
about Christianity had taken place with a wide
range of people, from girls attending the local
finishing schools to local residents who had lived in
the area for years. A children's Bible class had been
started, and a local government official who had
many questions eventually became a Christian. It
seemed as though God had a long list of tasks for
them to do in Champéry.

They returned to a heavy work load, serious
family sickness (Franky contracted polio on the trip
back to Switzerland), and exciting possibilities for
the future. At the end of 1954, the Schaeffers,
reflecting on the numbers of young people and
others who had brought their questions about Christianity to the chalet in Champéry, had the vision of
a ministry that would serve the increasing number
of people needing spiritual help. They decided to
rename their chalet to mark this new direction.
'Let's call it *L'Abri*,' suggested Francis – the name
is French for 'shelter' – 'and let these people know

that they are welcome to come back and bring friends with them.'[8]

One day in January 1955 Edith Schaeffer read Isaiah 2:2 and marked the verse in her Bible: 'Promise – yes, L'Abri.'

And then in February, everything changed.

The official communication evicting them from the canton of Valais and requiring them to leave Switzerland within six weeks gave as grounds for the ruling the fact that the family had had 'a religious influence in the village of Champéry'. Obviously the conversion of the local dignitary and the children's Bible class had been badly received, and their visitors' permits had been revoked.

The miraculous story of how they were able to find and purchase Chalet les Mélèzes in Huémoz, Vaud, has been told in Edith Schaeffer's *L'Abri*. It was a miracle of timing, of financial provision, and of timely advice. In due course the family moved, and a residency permit was granted.

CHALET les Mélèzes was to become famous all over the world, and thousands of people young and old would make the journey up the mountainside, coming from all over the world. Some were Christians, coming to L'Abri as a last resort, to see whether they might find out here whether Christianity really could give adequate answers to all the questions that their parents and churches were telling them were unspiritual. Others were not Christians but had heard that there was a place in Huémoz where you could get food and shelter and talk about religion. Some were artists, some scientists, some students, some teachers, some famous, the majority unknown.

They were coming to what was unique among residential Christian centres. Firstly in its administration; L'Abri from the beginning operated on the same four principles that it follows today. They would not appeal for money, but would make their needs known only to God. They would not advertise for staff, but would trust God to send the workers they needed at the right time. They would not make long-term plans, but would allow God to be sovereign in his guidance. And they would not advertise L'Abri, but would trust God to send the people whom he wanted to be there. The Schaeffers did not urge these principles on to others. But they believed that for them it was how God wanted the work to continue.

Secondly, it was unique as an environment. The Schaeffers liked to talk of visitors being 'in' L'Abri, not 'at' L'Abri. It was not a conference centre, and there was no students' lounge or other rooms for guests to congregate in on their own. Visitors stayed with a family; at first with the Schaeffers themselves, then as the work grew, also with the various additional workers and their families. They were expected to be guests as if they were staying

with friends or relatives; so the discussion at mealtimes involved everybody, and individual conversations, which would have caused the group to
fragment into several independent discussions, were
discouraged. Mealtimes, indeed, became a very
important part of the work, as guests brought their
questions or raised points from what they had been
reading or studying in the day. Then as now, a
L'Abri meal tended to be a lengthy event. Many of
those who came to Huémoz were from broken or
unloving homes, and Edith Schaeffer taught that a
meal table prepared with love and set out beauti-
fully was as much an expression of Christian truth
as was a theology book.[9]

The basis of L'Abri as a Christian ministry was
a willingness to answer questions. In the earliest
days the discussions took place between the family
and a handful of visitors. As more and more people
came, some questions were often asked and a
number of basic issues were dealt with over and
over again with different visitors. At an early stage,
it was decided to tape the discussions so that visitors could cover some ground on their own and
make the best use of the limited discussion time.
Schaeffer was initially rather reluctant to do this,
but became convinced that the advantages out-
weighed the disadvantages; from then on, every
significant lecture, seminar or discussion was taped.
Today, the L'Abri tape library contains tapes by
several generations of L'Abri workers, visiting

speakers and L'Abri associates, covering topics ranging from biblical perspectives on economics to the novels of Walker Percy and taking in on the way such areas as Bible studies, apologetics, philosophy, and relationships.

Many observers mistakenly concluded that L'Abri was a ministry exclusively to intellectuals and students. But though that was an important strand in the work from the beginning, it was only a strand; L'Abri functioned as much on the level of family relationships as it did on that of philosophical absolutes, and over the years many visitors who never listened to a L'Abri tape or opened a L'Abri book have been touched and convinced by the demonstration of the reality of God in everyday relationships, or by the welcoming, caring family homes of the L'Abri workers. Among those helped in this way have been drug addicts, victims of abuse, people contemplating suicide, and many more.

IT is not the purpose of this chapter to talk about what L'Abri became; that remarkable story is told in *L'Abri*, *The Tapestry* and elsewhere. In the 1960s it was already a pioneering mission to all who had abandoned the hope that Christianity could have anything relevant to say in answer to the hard questions posed by twentieth-century thought, culture, science and art. It was Schaeffer, for example,

who urged Christian parents to look at, instead of
dismissing, what their children were listening to
and being challenged by. He pointed out that among
the many voices speaking in contemporary culture,
some were asking questions that deserved an answer.

It was not, he said, that the Christian church did
not know the answers, but that the church often did
not know the questions. And the Christianity taught
by many churches was overlaid with irrelevancies:
for example, an insistence on certain social conventions, or a purely secular definition of success and
achievement. In a period of growing secular concern for the environment and the safety of the
planet, Schaeffer pointed out that many churches
were abusing the environment, not least aestheti-
cally. At a time when a generation was rebelling
against materialism, and the hippie movement was
urging a return to spiritual realities, the church was
often the most materialistic phenomenon in a Christian's life.

Students arrived fresh from grappling with the
ideas of McLuhan, Sartre, Camus, Heidegger and
more; Schaeffer, whose detailed knowledge of philosophical texts tended to suffer from his remote-
ness from universities and academic libraries, nevertheless offered a view of the history of ideas that
defended the biblical framework of truth yet was
capable of addressing and rebutting the arguments
of twentieth-century unbelief. Some who benefited

from his teaching went on to become prominent apologists themselves – for example, Clark Pinnock and Os Guinness. Hundreds now working in the arts, in science, in sociology and other disciplines acknowledge the influence of L'Abri in their development as Christian scholars (one professor once remarked to me, 'I would not call myself a Schaefferite: but the world *did* turn upside down when I met him, and it hasn't gone back the same way since ...').

It was, however, a crucial strand in his thinking that philosophy was not just something that belonged to the lecture room and learned books. Philosophical ideas 'filtered down', so that the person in the street before long had absorbed the essence of what was being taught in the universities. He drew widely from contemporary music, books, television programmes and cinema to make his point. A Schaeffer lecture might be based on a best-selling popular novel as easily as on a theological or philosophical publication. He made extensive use of *Time* and *Newsweek* articles in his teaching; academics who smiled at this practice misunderstood his point, for he was arguing that this was the form and the medium by which people absorbed the ideas of their time.

IN this developing, pioneering ministry, the Schaeffers listened as much as they talked. Their close friend Hans Rookmaaker, the Dutch art historian from Amsterdam who taught them much about art, was fond of quoting a line by Bob Dylan when lecturing to 'bourgeois' Christian audiences: 'Something is happening here, but you don't know what it is – do you, Mr Jones?'

The Schaeffers knew. They knew because they had listened to the voices of their culture, and had read and listened and watched far more widely than most – and this in a home that was not dominated by television and which, in its mountain solitude, was not well placed to keep a watching eye on what was being done and said in the world. But they listened to those who came up the mountain road from Aigle to the chalet in Huémoz: to the scholars, the farmers, the engineers, the school-leavers, the nurses, the artists and many more. Had they merely dispensed the gospel without pausing to listen first, the Schaeffers would have been faithful in pointing people to Christ but would never have acquired that understanding of people that made their ministry unique.

L'Abri grew as seekers arrived in Huémoz, often as a last resort because they had heard that here was a place to which they could bring honest questions and receive biblical answers that made sense. Many who recall the teaching they received there remember the Schaeffers weeping as they tended the scars that secular thinking had inflicted. The tears did not grow less as the years went by and the ministry tended to reflect the crises of the surrounding world: in the 1960s there was a great emphasis on the arts, just as in previous decades much apologetics had wrestled with Christianity and science. As the 1960s gave way to the 1970s, the focus shifted to more sociological matters – Schaeffer was one of the first to point out how the dreams of the sixties had now translated to a quest for 'personal peace and affluence'. In the 1970s a film, *How Then Shall We Live?*, directed by his son Franky and written and presented by Schaeffer, summarised his historical apologetic; a second, made in 1979 in conjunction with the US Surgeon-General Everett C. Koop and entitled *Whatever Happened to the Human Race?* addressed pro-life issues. In his final years Schaeffer was an international campaigner for the rights of the unborn, and, following the principles of Samuel Rutherford in *Lex Rex* (1644), strongly argued the case for civil disobedience in cases where governments had departed so far from biblical morality that a 'point of no return' had been reached.

Together with Edith, he was a prophetic spokesman on many issues, including freedom, political tyranny, the role and dignity of the family, the purity of the church and the sanctity of life. His creed of 'co-belligerence' gave him a shared platform with figures such as Malcolm Muggeridge and Mother Teresa. In all that he did he emphasised his central theme: that Christ must be Lord of the whole of life, that there were no 'safe areas' outside the ambit of his reign, that there was no area of life or thought that could escape the searchlight of his mind and his word.

As a philosopher and apologist, his influence was often tied to historical contexts that have now changed beyond recognition – Jean-Paul Sartre's ideas and the Communist ideology are two philosophies that no longer exercise the same dominance on thought. But the central apologetic, the Bible-based defence of truth, remains as valid as ever, and the thousands of visitors who have passed through L'Abri since his death testifies to the enduring value of the work. It is as a pastor and evangelist that he will be best remembered, however. He was a man who saw the hurt of the twentieth century more clearly than most, who was not ashamed to weep side by side with those who wept, and who was convinced of the validity and supreme effectiveness of the historic, orthodox, biblical faith to answer and rebuff the challenges of twentieth-century unbelief.

He summed himself up best. When a visitor once asked him whether he was a theologian or a philosopher, he replied, 'Neither. I'm just a simple old-fashioned evangelist.'

Notes

1. Francis Schaeffer, *Here We Stand* (Independent Board for Presbyterian Foreign Missions, Pa., [1948]), p.26.

2. *Ibid.*, p.35.

3. Francis Schaeffer, ed. Lane T. Dennis, *Letters of Francis Schaeffer* (Crossway, 1985), p. 39.

4. Francis A. Schaeffer, *The Church Before the Watching World* (Inter-Varsity Press, Ill., 1971), p.79.

5. These events are recorded in Ned B. Stonehouse, *J. Gresham Machen: a Biographical Memoir* (Westminster Theological Seminary, 3rd edn 1978). Two comprehensive studies are George Marsden, *Reforming Fundamentalism* (Eerdmans, 1987), and a publication of the Orthodox Presbyterian Church, *Pressing Towards the Mark* (The Committee for the Historian of the Orthodox Presbyterian Church, 1986).

6. Francis A. Schaeffer, *True Spirituality* (Hodder & Stoughton, 1971).

7. Francis Schaeffer, ed. Lane T. Dennis, *op. cit.*, p.33.

8. Edith Schaeffer, *L'Abri* (Norfolk Press, 1969), p.75.

9. She has developed this theme in several books, notably *Hidden Art* (Norfolk Press, 1972).

10

The Stand of Laszlo Tokes
The Courage of a Pastor
and his Church

The weather was unusually warm for most of that December day. Months later, when the world had been transformed out of all recognition and everything was very different, people would look back on that extraordinary time and acknowledge the unlikely role that the weather had played.

For the local people venturing out into the bleakness of the early morning twilight, the streets were chilly from the hours of darkness. But you had to be out early to get a good place in the queues. It was several hours before the shops would open, but there was no point in arriving later. Food was scarce. Husbands took their place in lines of shivering people, keeping a place for their wives to take over later when the men went off to work. There were sporadic conversations but for the most part people stood in silence. Nobody smiled much. Smiles were rare enough in Ceausescu's Romania.

It was 15 December 1989. In Timisoara, an obscure town in the south-west of the country near the Yugoslavian border, the grip of the harsh winter and the even harsher regime seemed to be as tight and deadening as ever.

INSIDE the Hungarian Reformed Church, Pastor
Laszlo Tokes and his family were preparing for the
new day. The pastor's rooms were only slightly less
cold than the streets outside; there had been little
fuel for the stoves that normally kept them warm.
The church occupied most of an imposing building,
its entrance in a quiet sidestreet with a stone staircase inside climbing up to the church entrance on
the top landing. The pastor's front door was on a
half-landing. There had been Securitate officers
stationed on the stairs for many days now, ostensibly to protect the family, but in reality to ensure that
their movements and those of their friends could be
carefully watched.

It had been a long and troubled journey from
Laszlo's childhood in Cluj to the post he now held
in Timisoara. Born into a large family of Hungarians, he grew up aware both of his own heritage as
a Hungarian citizen of Romania and of the growing
ethnic tensions that were being skilfully aggravated by Ceausescu. His father had been a deputy
bishop in the Hungarian Reformed Church, but had
lost his post for speaking out against the regime.
Laszlo entered the ministry too, training at the one
theological academy allowed by the regime, under
the teaching of barely-educated and unbelieving
lecturers who had been installed by the regime and
had gradually replaced the older, godly staff. At
college he became part of a circle of students who
cherished a deep ambition to reform the church,

planning to do so by building pockets of godly resistance in whatever church districts they were eventually assigned to.

It was a country that had experienced centuries of ethnic mixing. Once a Roman province, it bore the marks of the victorious Turks, the Austro-Hungarian empire and several more conquerors. More recently, the region of Transylvania had been taken from Hungary (considered a party to German aggression in the Second World War), and allocated to Romania in the post-war treaties. With it had come a large Hungarian population. The treaties lost Hungary two-thirds of its territory, and the ethnic bitterness that resulted had been aggravated by a policy of forced assimilation imposed by Ceausescu by which Hungarian communities in Transylvania were broken up and Romanian communities moved into the Transylvanian territories. Laszlo, his family and friends spoke Hungarian and called their towns by Hungarian names: Cluj was Kolozsvar, Timisoara was Temesvar, Oradea was Nagyvarad; but you could not buy a modern map with those names printed on it, and Hungarian was taught only in the few Hungarian schools. The two Hungarian universities in Transylvania were closed, Hungarian cultural activities such as travelling theatres were banned, and speaking Hungarian was restricted.

There were no winners in Ceausescu's territorial shuffles. Many Romanians suffered as much as

Hungarians did. Other minorities – including the large German population and the gypsy communities – also suffered, as Ceausescu's plan to weaken any social grouping that might conceivably become a threat to him climaxed in the appalling programme of 'systemisation', in which whole villages were to be razed to the ground and their residents moved into large residential complexes in the cities.

All that lay ahead when Laszlo Tokes entered upon his life's work as a pastor, going first as a junior assistant to Brasov in the heart of Romania where he spent two years working in a region where large German evangelical communities still flourished as a legacy of the days of the Austro-Hungarian domination. From there he went in 1977 to Dej, where he was appointed an assistant pastor.

Laszlo embarked upon a full programme of activities, including considerable work with young people. He organised Bible studies and discussion groups, often drawing on his experience as a child holidaying in a country village where the people's faith was expressed as much in their daily work as in their Sunday churchgoing. It was in that village that he had first realised that a biblical faith must inevitably affect every part of one's life, that Christianity could not be shut away in church to be taken out on Sundays but should actually shape the way one related to people, harvested one's fields, and viewed the world in which one lived.

So at Dej he encouraged the young people to consider what impact being a Christian ought to have on one's understanding of art, of science, of politics. What did the Bible have to say about injustice, about music, about philosophy? He encouraged the young people to analyse these questions, and to analyse themselves, too; sometimes one member of the group would volunteer to be cross-examined by the others about his or her faith, opinions, likes and dislikes. On other occasions he would announce that on one night a week, all discussions would be in English to improve their knowledge of foreign languages.

To many churches and Christian organisations in the West, such activities are hardly unusual. Most of the wealth of printed material we possess about how to lead youth groups and organise young peoples' activities in churches recommends doing exactly what Laszlo was doing. They point out how important it is that young people should understand that Christianity does have something to say about issues wider than Sunday School stories. There is a long tradition, too, of organisations such as the UCCF and Scripture Union, publications such as *Christianity Today* and *Third Way*, centres such as L'Abri Fellowship and Christian Impact in London, pressure groups such as CARE and the Evangelical Alliance, and special interest groups such as the Arts Centre Group and the Medical Christian Fellowship ... the list is endless.

In Ceausescu's Romania in the late 1970s, such riches were unimaginable. Had they been available, they would have been regarded by the regime as seditious. As it was, Laszlo's pioneering efforts brought him very quickly to the attention of the local Securitate officials. One of the most feared secret police systems in Europe, it was refined by Ceausescu into a superbly efficient information network that both ensured nothing could happen in Romania that escaped the eyes and ears of the regime, and that the people lived in permanent fear. Anybody could turn out to be an informer, and a casual comment or angry accusation made in the privacy of a small group at home or work might very well be in a report on the local police chief's desk within days. So thoroughly was the security network woven into Romanian life that even today, five years after the fall of Ceausescu, much of the structure and many of the officials are still in place.

Four weeks after his arrival in Dej, Laszlo was summoned to the local Securitate headquarters where he was shown a dossier recording his activities and public sermons since he began as a theological student.

'Your reputation has preceded you, Mr Tokes,' the official said coldly.

Laszlo realised that the only way the information could have reached the regime was through spies and informers among the staff and students of the theological academy.

THERE was constant harassment during the years in Dej, and the young people too were kept under observation and harassed in their turn. In the local cultural centre Laszlo enjoyed the limited opportunities for Hungarian drama, dance and music; he helped in the administration and arranged occasional poetry readings. But the authorities stepped in. He was ordered to reduce his involvement, and the centre itself came under attack. The students he had helped and the young people in his church groups were brought in to Securitate headquarters for questioning.

The greatest sorrow for Laszlo was that his bishop, Gyula Nagy, did not support him or the young people of the churches under his authority, but collaborated with the regime. 'He lived during one of the great crises of the Church,' Laszlo recalls, 'and he failed to make a stand.' The young people of Dej were entitled to the support of their bishop and did not receive it; and their assistant pastor was being harassed by the authorities (including Bishop Nagy) for doing no more than any pastor should do: making the Bible relevant to the people, demonstrating the relevance of Christianity to the questions and issues of everyday life, preaching a seamless integrity between faith and life, between living and believing. For the Ceausescu regime, it was a declaration of open war, in the same way that many believers in Romania had set themselves against the authorities not by choice, but because following Christ inevitably forced innumerable conflicts with the secular state.

Laszlo's confrontations with the state continued, always on the grounds that he and the church were being prevented from carrying out their proper duties. Replacing worn-out Bibles and hymnbooks was almost impossible. Young people could not be invited to evangelistic meetings. The ancient churches were falling into decay because repairs were impossible. Fewer and fewer trainee clergy were accepted, and those who succeeded in gaining a place at the academy were taught by inadequate teachers. Laszlo began a campaign of letter-writing, and also wrote occasional articles for an underground newspaper published by college friends.

WHEN matters came to a head in 1984 and Laszlo was summoned to appear before a disciplinary committee, it was the letters that formed the basis of the regime's case. The Dej church, surprisingly supported by Gyula Nagy, had elected him as full pastor, but the regime refused to allow it, producing ever more slender reasons. After a prolonged battle with the authorities, Laszlo lost his case, was dismissed from his post, and returned home to the family home in Cluj.

Every day for two years he donned his clerical clothes and waited outside the bishop's office. To everybody who asked what he was doing, he replied: 'I am a pastor in the Hungarian Reformed Church who has been denied a post.' He also attended conferences and attempted to make statements at question-time, and was threatened with arrest.

During this period he married Edit, whose family lived in the Dej region; acknowledging her support and encouragement during those years, he often reflected that her example had shown him how his mother had helped his father to endure the opposition and hatred of the regime during his own struggles with the regime. During these years, too, many voices were raised in the West against the treatment dissidents were receiving in Romania; Laszlo (who has often paid tribute to others of all ethnic backgrounds who suffered far greater persecution than himself) was the subject of protests by American politicians and others. It was almost certainly the Western protests, and Ceausescu's pragmatism – he cherished the American award of Most Favoured Nation status – that led to Laszlo being appointed, in 1986, as assistant to Pastor Leo Peuker in the distant town of Timisoara, a place sufficiently remote for this turbulent priest to be buried in obscurity.

NOBODY knows what thoughts passed through Laszlo Tokes's mind as he removed the boards from his broken study window and looked out at nine o'clock

on that fateful morning of 15 December 1989.
Perhaps he reflected how long it had been before he
and Edit had been allowed the luxury of their own
apartment; for months they had lived, on Peuker's
orders, in a cupboard-like room leading off the
main church hall, despite pleas that they should be
allowed to use some of the empty rooms in the
building for accommodation for themselves and
their new baby, Maté. Perhaps, on this mid-December
morning, he remembered the Christmas sermon
preached by Peuker on 'No room at the inn'; Maté's
fretful wailing had been audible through the thin
door of their tiny room and echoed round the
congregation.

Most likely, as he looked out across the street to
the building on the other side of the street from
where Securitate spies had been watching him for
weeks, he wondered exactly how the authorities
would make their move. For this was the day on
which he was to be forcibly removed from his post
and exiled to Mineu, a village in the hills of Northern Romania, reached only by dirt tracks; an exile
that should certainly ensure that this time Laszlo
Tokes would be silenced and forgotten.

FOR the years at Timisoara had not worked out as
the authorities had hoped. The bishop to whom he
was now responsible, Laszlo Papp of Oradea, was
a much more committed collaborator with the

regime than Gyula Nagy had ever been, but Laszlo
had remained unimpressed by threats and cajoling.
That was why, when Pastor Peuker died suddenly
of a heart attack, Laszlo was not promoted to full
pastor; an assistant pastor was answerable directly
to the bishop in a way that a full pastor was not, and
Bishop Papp wanted to keep this young dissident
under his eye. Hints were dropped that if Laszlo
behaved himself, there were no limits to how high
he could rise. Laszlo ignored the hints and set
himself to rebuilding the dispirited and shattered
church in Timisoara.

The congregation increased dramatically, and
in the city news spread of the tall Hungarian with
the deep bass voice, whose sermons challenged the
church to rebuild itself, to be a bulwark in times of
persecution. He was building not an organisation
but a family: 'I am not the only pastor here,' he told
his church. 'We must all be pastors to each other.'
Soon a building programme began to extend the
church. The numbers of baptisms increased; work
with young people expanded; the Securitate watched
and took notes, often sending spies into the congregation itself during sermons.

Bishop Papp summoned Laszlo to his office and
rebuked him, calling him self-seeking and proud,
but Laszlo made the same answer he had made to
every criticism the regime had ever made of him:
that he was only doing what pastors should do. He
was only working to build the church and teach his

people from the Word of God. Why was the bishop opposing him? Was a pastor not entitled to the support and encouragement of his ecclesiastical superiors?

When in 1988 the systemisation programme (and with it the planned destruction of villages and village churches) became known in Romania, Laszlo and some of his friends in the church campaigned to persuade all the churches to resist it. Few churches in the diocese were prepared to join the campaign, and Laszlo and his colleagues were hauled before Bishop Papp and given an official warning. Shortly afterwards Laszlo was summoned to the office of the local Inspector of Cults, the government department controlling religious matters, to answer an anonymous charge of mismanagement of the church, nationalism and incitement against the state. Afterwards, Laszlo wrote to Bishop Papp in Oradea requesting his support against state persecution, but Papp responded with further rebukes. It was clear that far from being buried in obscurity in Timisoara, Laszlo had placed himself in direct confrontation with Ceausescu's regime and its puppet, Bishop Laszlo Papp.

Laszlo continued to look for ways to build up his church. He recognised that all the churches were facing similar problems; Ceausescu sometimes favoured one rather than the rest and gave it special privileges, but it was a cynical way of fuelling resentment between the ethnic communities and

their churches. Laszlo decided to initiate joint activities with some of the neighbouring congregations, and arranged the first with the predominantly
German Roman Catholic Church. The ecumenical
festival service, incorporating German and Hungarian music and literature in the worship, was a
great success, and many of the leading intellectuals
of Timisoara accepted invitations to attend.

It was hardly surprising that Laszlo should find
Timisoara a good place to launch such a scheme.
The city and the region were notable in Romania for
their exceptional ethnic harmony. Timisoara had
been ruled by many states through the centuries and
its residents rubbed shoulders tolerantly. In the
cities of central Transylvania, like Tirgu-Mures
and Sibiu, the forced movements of population had
left a harvest of resentment. In Cluj, the old Hungarian districts had been largely demolished and
rebuilt. But Timisoara had a greater measure of
integration.

Encouraged by the success of the joint service
Laszlo invited the nearby Orthodox Church to join
him in the next. But the Securitate had already
taken steps to quash the new venture. More severe
harassment than ever before was directed at the
churches and those who had taken part, many of
them students who now found their education in
jeopardy. A diocesan church official forbade further attempts to attract young people to the church,
and the warning was reinforced by an edict from

Bishop Papp that even banned the formation of church choirs. No more was heard from the Orthodox Church about a joint service, and it was obvious that its clergy had received threats from the Securitate.

Gradually, the regime and the corrupt church administration of Bishop Papp's diocese of Oradea succeeded in isolating Laszlo. One of his closest supporters in the anti-systemisation campaign suddenly found a long-standing request to leave the country inexplicably granted. Another was forced to move with his family to a bitterly anti-Hungarian region of the diocese. Laszlo's congregation continued to support him in the face of many disappointments and discouragements; the authorities forbade them to continue with the church building programme, and many individuals found the usual frustrations of life suddenly increased sharply.

When Bishop Papp's patience ran out, he moved decisively. Laszlo would be required to leave his post and take a pastorate in Mineu. The decision was rushed through by an illegally-constituted church committee. Laszlo refused to go, and announced that he would begin a voluntary house-arrest in protest.

CONDITIONS in Romania were worsening, after several harsh winters and Ceausescu's brutal economies that left the people little food and heat. During the months of protest, Laszlo and his church distributed food and other supplies that were brought in, often at considerable risk, by foreign visitors. The spectacle of the dictator's ludicrous palace in Bucharest, built on the site of acres of the beautiful old city that had been destroyed to make room for it, contrasted cruelly with the suffering of the people living in shoddily-built apartments along rubbled streets, among the ruins of communities that had been bulldozed. The shops were empty, apart from the smart boutiques in the large cities where the privileged members of the regime chose trinkets from abroad. The last days of the Ceausescus continued the crazy pantomime that would have been comic were it not so costly in human lives: when Nicolae and Elena Ceausescu relaxed in their rural retreats, he shot wildly at boars that had to be almost tied down so that the dictator could not miss, and his wife enjoyed her reputation as an international scientist, surrounded by volumes of her 'research papers' written by underlings. It was common (if dangerous) knowledge in the scientific community that Elena could not understand the simplest undergraduate textbook.

Yet silence prevailed. The people of Romania were afraid, with good reason. There was a wall of silence that hid the evil of the regime from the outside world. Laszlo planned to demolish it.

IN July 1989, a Hungarian news programme that was seen throughout a large part of Romania broadcast an interview with Laszlo. It had been filmed, secretly and at great risk, in March, just before the Bishop gave him notice to quit. Laszlo, filmed inside his church, spelt out to the outside world what was happening in his country. 'The wall of silence is more solid and impenetrable than the Berlin Wall,' he said soberly. 'Somebody should knock it down.'

After the broadcast, in a last appeal to Bishop Papp he urged him to resign or to change his policies. Papp responded curtly: if he did not leave Timisoara, he would be forcibly evicted. It was a completely illegal ruling. Only a church could evict its pastor. Bishop Papp could only have made the threat if he knew he had the full weight of Ceausescu's regime to back him up.

Pressure on the church grew horrifically. A much-loved member of the congregation who had led the building programme and spoken out against the attempts to remove Laszlo was found dead in mysterious circumstances that pointed ominously to murder. The church verger received such frightening threats from the Securitate that he could not come to work. One night four thugs burst into Laszlo's apartment and attacked Laszlo with a knife as Edit and Maté managed to find shelter in a bedroom. On another occasion hooligans smashed all the windows. It was clear that telephones were being tapped, and there was plentiful evidence that they were being spied on constantly. Police guards were stationed outside the apartment and the congregation was forbidden to bring food or other help to the family, but they found ways round the ban, often risking injury or arrest.

By early December, Bishop Papp had managed to procure the documents that gave some semblance of legality to the eviction. The date was set for 15 December. Laszlo told his congregation. 'It is illegal,' he said to them. 'I want you to come to the church on that day and observe what happens. This must not happen without witnesses. Come and watch.' Maté, for safety, was sent to stay with Laszlo's parents in Cluj.

As Laszlo looked out of the window on the morning of 15 December he saw that they had come. In the street outside and in the main road beyond, at least thirty or forty people stood in small groups, their breath curling in the crisp air.

The story of that extraordinary day, and the day that followed, became well-known all over the world, and Laszlo has told it himself in his autobiography.[1] The Securitate watched helplessly as the crowd grew outside the church, first the Hungarian congregation, then joined by Romanians, Germans, gypsies and other minorities, as news spread that in the Hungarian church a pastor was defying the might of the regime. Laszlo preached to them from the window, and they sang hymns and songs together. Inside, the local authorities tried desperately to negotiate with Laszlo. The town mayor arrived, declared himself shocked by Laszlo's problems and promised that the broken windows would be mended and other grievances dealt with. 'We have no links with the Securitate,' he said smoothly, 'and we do not know why the bishop has done these things. But we know you are a good man ...' By dusk, there had been many visitors to the pastor's apartment. The people outside were massed several deep, holding candles, shouting encouragement to Laszlo. Eventually he persuaded them to go to their homes. By one o'clock, only a few people remained. Long afterwards, he discovered that the police had cleared the street by force, sending in plain clothes men armed with clubs.

AMONG the early visitors next day was the family doctor. Edit was several months pregnant and had not slept for six nights. Half an hour later the mayor arrived with three doctors who examined her and said that she must be moved to hospital. On the advice of the family doctor, the Tokeses refused. It was a transparent attempt to divide and conquer.

The crowd, building up again outside the building, was amazed not long afterwards to see firewood being delivered and a glazier repairing the broken windows. Glass was unobtainable in Timisoara, and firewood scarce. Laszlo went to the window. The weather was bright and sunny, and it was a Saturday; the streets were full of people. Had it been a typical Romanian December day, most of them would have been huddled by their stoves at home.

'Thank you in God's name for coming,' he said. 'You see the mayor has done what he promised. We have gained what we wanted. It's dangerous for you to stay here. Please, go to your homes.' But the crowd refused to go. Laszlo explained that the mayor had promised that there would be no eviction, but they demanded written proof.

It was a turning-point. Laszlo had not asked for a demonstration. He had only asked for witnesses. But the sight of the Securitate holding back as a church pastor and his congregation quietly demanded their rights as citizens and believers inspired many in the crowd to believe the unbelievable; that perhaps today was the day when the long silence could be broken, when a stand against the dictator could be made. That was the point when the crowd, for the first time, began to sing the Romanian nationalist songs that Ceausescu had long since outlawed.

In a sense, Laszlo Tokes's role in the Romanian revolution ended that afternoon. Arrested that night and taken with Edit by force to Mineu, he was imprisoned for the rest of the events of that extraordinary week: the uprisings in Timisoara, in Arad, in other Romanian cities; the savage reprisals by the regime; the picture on the world's TV of the dictator's face frozen in fear, as the crowd before his palace booed and shouted 'Murderer! Timisoara!' at him; the flight of the Ceausescus, their arrest, their execution.

Laszlo was not the only dissident, either. When he was nominated for the Nobel peace prize that year he was jointly nominated with Professor Doina Cornea, a prominent and courageous critic of the regime.

He was, moreover, an unlikely spark for a revolution. A member of the Hungarian minority, after the revolution he was frequently vilified and threatened by Romanian nationalists, and there is today ample evidence that some of the threats against him before the revolution are still in place. In 1992, an illegal people's court placed a price of $150,000 on his head, and charges against him in parliament of anti-Romanian activities sounded suspiciously like the old Securitate charges brought against him in Dej and Timisoara. There is no longer a price on his head, but he and the Hungarian minority have continued to suffer loss of human, civil and religious rights in a Romania that is still troubled and often shackled by the past.

So why Laszlo Tokes?

The answer is simple. Throughout his long and
dangerous confrontation with the Ceausescu regime and its ecclesiastical puppets, his demands
were always the same. He insisted on the right of
the church to go about its business, on the duty of a
bishop to nurture his flock, on the duty of a state to
protect freedom of belief. He campaigned for the
protection of church buildings, for the provision of
adequate hymn books, for the training of adequate
clergy. He did not seek to topple a regime. He just
wanted to be a pastor and get on with his work,
especially with young people.

Many brilliant politicians and courageous revo-
lutionaries tried to topple the Ceausescu regime
and failed. Ceausescu's path to that comical palace
on the Revolution Boulevard in Bucharest is lit-
tered with the political (and sometimes the actual)
corpses of his rivals. But when God brought the
tyrant down, he chose to use as the spark not a
popular hero nor a master strategist, but an obscure
minister in a minority church.

There can have been few revolutions begun by
a pastor insisting on holding Bible classes.

Note

1. Laszlo Tokes with David Porter, *With God, For the People*
(Hodder & Stoughton, 1990).

Background Notes and Suggestions for Further Reading

Augustine

Augustine's many writings are listed in a number of sources; for example, the articles in reference books such as *The Oxford Dictionary of the Christian Church* have extensive bibliographies. The texts I have used for this chapter are those selected, translated and edited by Albert C. Outler, John Burnaby and John H. S. Burleigh ('The Library of Christian Classics' vols vi, vii, viii; SCM Press, 1953-1955). There are good translations of *The Confessions* and *The City of God* available in Penguin. Valuable anthologies of Christian texts are Henry Bettenson, *The Early Christian Fathers* and *The Later Christian Fathers* (both OUP, 1956 and 1970).

General histories of the early church give helpful background; a popular account by a noted historian is Henry Chadwick, *The Early Church* (Penguin, 1967). This, too, has a thorough bibliography. Also useful is Gerald Bray, *Creeds, Councils and Christ* (IVP, 1984); an interesting view from the Orthodox Church on the Augustinian controversies is provided in Timothy Ware, *The Orthodox Church* (Penguin Books, rev edn 1993). Biographies of Augustine include Gerald Bonner, *St Augustine of Hippo* (Canterbury Press, 2nd edn 1986); Peter Brown, *Augustine of Hippo: A Biogra-*

phy (Faber & Faber, 1967); and Henry Chadwick, *Augustine* (OUP, 1986). An assessment from an older tradition is that by B. B. Warfield, whose writings on Augustine from the early years of this century are collected in *Studies in Tertullian and Augustine* (1930: repr as vol 4 of *Works*, Baker Book House, 1981).

Martin Luther

Luther has the distinction of being the subject of more books than anybody else except Jesus Christ. I have found the biographies by Kittelson and Atkinson to be both readable and helpful; for details, see the footnotes. Older accounts are still often illuminating; R. Bainton's *Here I Stand* (1950) and A. G. Dickens, *Martin Luther and the Reformation* (1967), for example. Luther's life should really be read alongside an introduction to mediaeval thought and theology; one helpful discussion is G. Rupp, *The Righteousness of God* (1953). There is a useful bibliography in Kittelson. A valuable and readable context for Luther is provided in Maurice Keen, *The Pelican History of Mediaeval Europe* (1969), and Owen Chadwick's *The Reformation* (1964) is as readable and thorough as are all the volumes in the Pelican History of the Church. Heiko A. Oberman's *The History of the Reformation* (1994) includes an essay on the *via moderna* and two on Staupitz.

Extracts from Luther's voluminous writings are easily obtainable. Henry Bettenson, *Documents of the Christian Church* is a standard work: I have used the second edition, 1963.

Like many of the old communist countries (though sadly not all), the East German authorities took reasonably good care of many of their historic sites and much of interest still remains in Wittenberg and elsewhere. No doubt some enterprising travel agent will organise Luther tours, if they do not already exist!

John Bunyan

Pilgrim's Progress is one of the world's great books, but too many readers stop at the end of the First Part; the Second is an essential complement and contains its share of immortal characters. The Penguin edition of 1965 contains both parts, authoritatively edited and introduced by Roger Sharrock. An intriguing and evocative glimpse of how the book appeared to its first readers is provided by the Scolar Press facsimile edition of 1970.

The five major works are available from a variety of publishers and with varying amounts of editorial comment; for example, *Grace Abounding to the Chief of Sinners* is available with *The Pilgrim's Progress I & II* and *A Relation of the Imprisonment of Mr. John Bunyan* in the Oxford Standard Authors series (OUP, 1966), again edited by Roger Sharrock, though without much by way of critical apparatus. My own edition of *The Holy War* (ed. David Porter, Christian Focus Publications, 1993) is based on the 1851 edition by George Offor; copies of Offor can still be found second-hand. Any good book shop or public library will be able to suggest further editions of Bunyan's many books, though the minor works will usually only be available in collected editions such as those available from time to time from American Christian publishers such as Baker (1977). Do not be tempted by a 'modernised' edition, except when buying a gift for a young child: Bunyan's virile and characterful prose is no more difficult than the Authorised Version of the Bible, though it is much more colloquial.

Bunyan's biographers, like those of many Christian leaders, sometimes tend to create the kind of Bunyan they think he should have been. Frank Mott Harrison's *John Bunyan* (1928: repr. Banner of Truth 1964) is an affectionate study by a devoted Bunyanite, but is too defensive to be reliable, does not relate Bunyan to his context very well, and is written in a style that you will either love or loathe. Harrison's *Bibliography of the Works of John Bunyan* (Trans. of the Bibliographical Society, 1932) is however well respected. He also revised the monumental biography by John Brown (4th edn 1902: Tercentenary edn, rev. Harrison, 1928), which is well worth consulting. Of more recent biographies, there is a wide choice including those by W. Y.

Tindall (1934), Roger Sharrock (1954), Ola Elizabeth Winslow (1961), Richard Greaves (1969), Monica Furlong (1975), and N. H. Keeble (1988).

Interested sightseers will find a trip to Bedford worthwhile; apart from historical monuments (including a Bunyan Museum in the Moot Hall) and Bunyan sites (sometimes of doubtful authenticity), there are a number of local landmarks which are thought to have inspired some of the scenery in *The Pilgrim's Progress*.

I cannot resist mentioning that, at the time of writing, Madame Tussaud's waxwork museum in London has two splendid life-sized models of Charles I and Oliver Cromwell. They are extremely perceptive studies, eerily evocative of their time, and to spend ten minutes contemplating them is to understand the seventeenth century a little better. A more conventional London pilgrimage would be to Bunhill Fields off City Road where Bunyan is buried; the area has a number of sites associated with the Puritans and with John Wesley, whose house and chapel are nearby.

John Wesley

I have made use of the Standard Edition of Wesley's *Journal* (from which most of the unacknowledged quotations are taken) and the classic biographies of John Wesley by Luke Tyerman, John Telford and Marjorie Bowen; I have also referred to

Telford's biography of Charles Wesley. All Wesley studies, however, have to be evaluated in the light of the flood of new material available in recent decades, including the final decoding of the shorthand cipher in which he wrote his private notes, the publication of the massively authoritative 'Bicentennial Edition', and a wealth of research into eighteenth-century pietism. Few books draw on this material as readably as does John Pollock's *John Wesley 1703-1791* (Hodder & Stoughton, 1989), which is strongly recommended as a starting point for further study.

Among other books I have found helpful are J. E. Rattenbury *The Conversion of the Wesleys* (Epworth Press, 1938), the bicentenary symposium *Wesley Studies* (Charles Kelly, n.d., c.1903), Arnold Dallimore *George Whitefield* (Vol. 1: Banner of Truth, 1970), A. Skevington Wood *The Inextinguishable Blaze* (Paternoster Press, 1960), Dorothy George *London Life in the Eighteenth Century* (Penguine Peregrine, 1966), and a number of early guides to London. There is a useful and scholarly collection of representative texts from Wesley's writings in *John Wesley*, ed. Albert C. Outler (Library of Protestant Thought: Oxford University Press, 1964).

Several London buildings associated with Wesley were destroyed or badly damaged in the Second World War. But many were later restored, for example the schools, Westminster and

Charterhouse; a walk with a good guidebook (particularly in the City Road area) will prove very rewarding. There is a sharp bend in Aldersgate Street (now a concrete wilderness), near the junction with Little Britain, that marks the site of Nettleton Court where Wesley's conversion probably took place.

In Epworth the church and rectory are worth visiting. In Bristol, the 'New Room' (Wesley's chapel in the Horsefair) is well restored; the small apartment there possesses an uncanny, timeless quality: as if Wesley left for a walk a few minutes before you arrived, and will be back at any moment.

David Livingstone

The history of African missions is told in many authoritative works, not least in the official archives and histories of Africa missionary societies. As a general guide, a reliable source (recommended more than once in the present book) is Stephen Neill's *A History of Christian Missions* (Penguin, 1964) which sets the evangelisation of Africa in a global and historical context. Among its useful pages are descriptions of the work of the London Missionary Society and an account of missions to China over 1,350 years, including those of the LMS. A notable collection of books and documents on Africa, including missionary material, is the Library of the Royal Commonwealth Society, now housed in the Cambridge University Library. The relationship between Christian mission and colonialism is very well described in Brian Stanley, *The Bible and the Flag* (IVP Apollos, 1990), which is a much more sympathetic – though unsparing – study than the sometimes hostile Julian Pettifer and Richard Bradley *Missionaries* (BBC, 1990).

Biographies of Livingstone divide into the adoring and the critical, though neither term is used here in a derogatory sense. The early biographies, and the accounts produced for children, belong to a long tradition of what is called 'hagiography' – exemplified by the 'saints' lives' written throughout the Christian era. These were designed to show the magnitude of God's grace in saving a wretched sinner (as in John Bunyan's *Grace Abounding to the Chief of Sinners*) or the unmistakable signs of God's seal upon a person from a very early age (as, for example, the 'plucking from the burning' episode in John Wesley's *Journal*, conscientiously edited by Wesley for maximum edification). Many early accounts of Livingstone belong to the latter category, emphasising the achievements of his childhood, the fact that from an early age he cherished an ambition to be a missionary, and the stoic heroism of his last years, the Africans bearing his body to the coast, and his eventual burial in Westminster Abbey. There is a sense in which the adoration in such biographies is not directed at Livingstone at all. Of the early biographies, the official account is W. G. Blaikie, *The Personal Life of David Livingstone* (London 1880). Blaikie was the only early biographer of Livingstone to have access to family archives and letters.

Later biographies came after a transformation in thinking about mission and an explosion of information and research about Africa (and about Livingstone), neither of which could be ignored by responsible scholars. The dismantling of the Livingstone hagiography and revaluation of his work have often seemed to be wrecking operations based on cynicism and dislike of Christianity. For example, Tim Jeal's centenary biography *Livingstone* (Heinemann, 1973) drew on a wide range of archives and documents and was rigorous in its scrutiny of the hagiography. He includes in his sources several post-war works which attempted a much more thorough analysis of Livingstone than had previously appeared. Jeal was convinced that Livingstone was a failure as a missionary and that his real achievements had been barely understood. Yet he is essentially sympathetic to Livingstone.

Another centenary publication is Bridglal Pachai (ed.), *Livingstone, Man of Africa: Memorial Essays 1873-1973* (Longman, 1973). Livingstone's own writings include *Missionary Travels and Researches in South Africa* (1857) and *The Zambesi and its Tributaries* (1865).

There is a Livingstone memorial in Blantyre, where his birthplace is preserved.

Dwight L Moody

According to Moody's son Will, the evangelist was asked by a friend in 1894 for permission to write the great man's biography. Moody declined, saying that he would prefer Will to be the author of the authorised biography after his father's death, and assuring his son that with the help of family friends the task would be straightforward. When Moody died, several authors announced that they intended to publish biographies, and Will published his account feeling that had there not been competition, he could have done a more thorough job.

It must have been frustrating for Will Moody, who had already seen several accounts published during D. L. Moody's lifetime; two in 1875 (if you include R. W. Clark's *The Work of God in Great Britain*), E. J. Goodspeed's account of Moody and Sankey published in 1876, and three further biographies in 1877. But Will Moody's biography *The Life of Dwight L. Moody* appeared in 1900 less than twelve months after his father's death, and it is after all only a measure of the man's reputation that five other biographies appeared in the same year.

Recent biographies include John Pollock's *Moody without Sankey* (Hodder & Stoughton, 1963) and J. F. Findlay's *Dwight L. Moody, American Evangelist, 1837-1899* (Chicago, 1969). So important was he in the history of evangelism that there are plentiful references to him in many books. Perhaps this is as good a place as any to commend

David L. Edwards' monumental *Christian England* (Collins Fount, rev. edn 1989), a revision of three earlier volumes; he sets a substantial assessment of Moody into a balanced historical context.

A major study of Victorian revivalism that acknowledges such parallel strands as the Anglo-Catholic initiatives is John Kent's *Holding the Fort* (Epworth Press, 1978), which devotes several chapters to Moody and Sankey. Disappointingly, two works which are invaluable for historical background to Moody's crusades – Alec R. Vidler, *The Church in an Age of Revolution* (Penguin, 1961) and Owen Chadwick, *The Victorian Church* (2 vols: A. & C. Black, 1966 and 1970) – have little specific to say about Moody.

For Moody's own writings, the bibliographies in Pollock and Findlay are a good starting point, and also describe the Moody archives in Northfield and in the Moody Bible Institute. There are numerous lesser memorials, for Moody and Sankey travelled extensively and were remembered with affection for years afterwards. In Liverpool as a young man I attended a businessmen's weekly prayer meeting in a room that housed a chair on which, it was said, Moody was known to have sat.

Sankey's music can be found easily enough second-hand, and John Kent, above, is an invaluable guide to his massive output. Its influence on Christian music generally and its relationship to secular music have been discussed in many places, as has Moody's introduction of the 'enquiry room' system.

Jim Elliot

The standard, and indispensable, biography of Jim Elliot is by his widow Elisabeth Elliot: *Shadow of the Almighty* (1958: currently O. M. Publishing, 1988). Her account of the five Ecuador martyrs, *Through Gates of Splendour* (1956: currently O. M. Publishing, 1980), is a modern missionary classic, and she has also edited *The Journals of Jim Elliot* (USA: Fleming H. Revell, 1978). The life of Nate Saint, the ingenious logistics expert of 'Operation Auca', is told in Russell T. Hitt, *Jungle Pilot* (Hodder & Stoughton, 1960).

Jim Elliot's name is honoured at Wheaton College today, but there are few sites preserved as memorials to him. There are plaques in the chapel and in Elliot Hall dormitory, some photographs preserved in the college archives, a collection of Jim Elliot documents in the Billy Graham Centre Archives, and a display of Auca-related photographs. He would not have wanted more. Nothing he wrote and nothing of his conversation that is recorded suggests that he would have wanted a public memorial. The enduring monument to the five Ecuador martyrs is to be found in the work that was built on theirs. Elisabeth Elliot wrote in 1958,

Jim left for me ... and for us all ... the testimony of a man who sought nothing but the will of God, who prayed that his life would be 'an exhibit to the value of knowing God'. The interest that accrues from this legacy is yet to be realised. It is hinted at in the lives of Quichua Indians who have determined to follow Christ, persuaded by Jim's example; in the lives of many who still write to tell me of a new desire to know God as Jim did.[1]

He would have wanted to add, as Elisabeth Elliot does in the preface to *Shadow of the Almighty*, that the word 'martyr' in the Bible is simply the word for 'witness'.

C S Lewis

An obvious source of further information is Lewis's 1955 autobiography *Surprised by Joy*. Of books *about* him, there are hundreds. Because C. S. Lewis is claimed by so many different traditions, it is a good idea to read more than one biography. I would recommend the biographies by A. N. Wilson (1990) and by Roger Lancelyn Green and Walter Hooper (1974); both are entitled *C. S. Lewis, a Biography*, make very different assessments, and the truth no doubt lies somewhere in between – though for my money it is slightly more in the direction of Wilson. Colin Duriez's *The C. S. Lewis Handbook* (Monarch, 1990), is a handy guide to Lewis's life and

1. *Shadow of the Almighty*, p.310.

work. Those contemplating long car journeys will enjoy the readings of the Narnia stories by Sir Michael Horden on cassette.

I suspect that my own lack of enthusiasm for pilgrimages to C. S. Lewis sites is one he would have shared, especially as such sites tend to be crowded with other pilgrims. You will get a better flavour of Lewis if you climb one of the hills near Oxford with an anthology of English verse in your pocket and read it at the top of your voice from the summit, though to reproduce Lewis's favourite outings you should really have a bottle of beer with you as well.

The Oxford and Cambridge that Jack knew have changed in few important respects, and you can track down the places associated with him easily enough. If you can afford it, you can take part in one of several Lewis gatherings on either side of the Atlantic. But it's easy to study him for yourself, for the books are easily obtained. An interesting hobby is seeking out first editions of his works in jumble sales and second-hand bookshops, though he had little interest in first editions or rare book collecting himself.

Francis Schaeffer

Francis Schaeffer's collected writings have been published as *The Complete Works of Francis Schaeffer: A Christian Worldview* (Crossway, Ill., 1982), but this is only half the story; the other half is to be found in Edith Schaeffer's *L'Abri* (Norfolk Press, 1969) and her extended autobiography of herself and her husband, *The Tapestry* (Word, Tx., 1981). The former is a vivid account of the earlier years of L'Abri; the latter is a huge rambling book full of detail. Three important books by Schaeffer have been published in a one-volume edition by IVP, and stocks of some out-of-print titles are held by L'Abri Fellowship at the address given below. An enjoyable account of one person's encounter with the Schaeffers during the Champéry years is the exuberant autobiography by Betty Carlson, *An Unhurried Chase to L'Abri* (Coverdale House UK, 1970). The author, whose conversion to Christianity is movingly described in the book, went on to live and work in L'Abri. Another encounter with L'Abri in the 1960s is to be found in *Arts And Minds: the Story Of Nigel Goodwin* (David Porter, Hodder and Stoughton, 1993).

The American theological background to L'Abri's beginnings is described by Schaeffer himself in *The Church Before the Watching World* (Inter-Varsity Press, Ill., 1970), which needs to be read in conjunction with the relevant *Letters*. The character of Gresham Machen, and the passionate concern for God's truth which drove him, is plain to see in *The Christian Faith in the Modern World* (Hodder & Stoughton, 1936), a moving defence of the historic biblical faith, based on radio talks given the year before he was 'unfrocked' for defending it. Some insight into another early influence on Schaeffer's apologetics, in fairly readable form, can be got from Cornelius Van Til, *The Reformed Pastor and Modern Thought* (USA: Presbyterian & Reformed, 1971).

There have been a number of books discussing Schaeffer's work. Some have been too uncritical to contribute much to an objective assessment of his remarkable ministry; others are more rigorous in their discussion but do not communicate the pastoral qualities which were the key to his apologetic methods. An example of the former is Louis G. Parkhurst, *Francis Schaeffer: the Man and his Message* (Tyndale, Ill., 1985); an example of the latter is a critical study published by a PhD student during Schaeffer's lifetime – Thomas V. Morris, *Francis Schaeffer's Apologetics* (Moody Bible Institute, Chicago, 1976). A good mix of personal reminiscence and academic assessment can be found in the contributions to Lane T. Dennis (ed.), *Francis A. Schaeffer: Portraits of the Man and His Work* (Crossway, Ill., 1986), to which Dennis contributes a good introduction. More academically orientated is Ronald W. Ruegsegger (ed.), *Reflections on Francis Schaeffer* (Zondervan, 1986), in which a number of practising academics critique aspects of Schaeffer's thought. It is a rigorously critical and deeply appreciative book, characterised by J. I. Packer's introductory tribute:

I am sure, however, that I shall not be at all wrong when I hail Francis Schaeffer, the little Presbyterian pastor who saw so much more of what he was looking at and agonized over it so much more tenderly than the rest of us, as one of the truly great Christians of my time.[2]

L'Abri Fellowship continues its work in several countries, and there is still a L'Abri community in Huémoz. In each of the L'Abri centres, people visit for the purpose of study and discussion. The basis of the work remains the same as it always has been: to demonstrate the reality of the God of the Bible, and to teach the adequacy of biblical Christianity to answer all the deep questions of modern men and women.

Information about the work of L'Abri and outside events such as occasional L'Abri Conferences, and also catalogues of L'Abri publications and the postal tape library can be obtained from the English branch, to whom requests to visit L'Abri should, in the first instance, be sent. Write to the Secretary at:

L'Abri Fellowship,
The Manor House
Greatham
Nr Liss, Hampshire GU33 6HF.
England UK.

---

2. Ronald W. Ruegsegger (ed.), *Reflections on Francis Schaeffer* (Zondervan, Mich., 1986), p.17.

Laszlo Tokes

I have based most of this chapter on my own experiences, travels and conversations in Romania since 1990, many of them with Laszlo Tokes and his family. Laszlo's biography and the story of December 1989 in Timisoara are told in much greater detail, and in his own words, in *With God, For the People* (Hodder & Stoughton, 1990), which I co-wrote with him. I have also told the story of a Christian literature and relief aid organisation extensively active in Romania and Eastern Europe in *Go Deliver! The Blythswood Story* (Christian Focus Publications, 1992).

Other sources of information can be found in issues of *Religion in Communist Lands*, the journal of Keston College, Oxford. Although overtaken by the events of 1989-90, Janice Broun's *Conscience and Captivity: Religion in Eastern Europe* (USA: Ethics and Public Policy Center; UK distrib., University Press of America) is an authoritative guide to the religious and general history of each of the Eastern European countries. A most moving account of a return to post-Ceausescu Romania is given in Richard Wurmbrand, *From Torture to Triumph* (Monarch, 1991). For an understanding of Laszlo's Hungarian background (and the history of Transylvania until recent times), two histories of Hungary are especially readable: Peter Hanak (ed.), *One Thousand Years: a Concise History of Hungary* (Budapest: Corvina, 1988), and Istvan Lazar's lavishly visual *An Illustrated History of Hungary* (Budapest: Corvina, 2nd edn 1990). Both should be available by order from good bookshops. A. J. P. Taylor's *The Hapsburg Monarchy 1809-1918* (1948: Penguin edn 1990) is a stimulating survey of the region's modern background.

Romania is not so difficult a country to visit as might at first appear, though facilities are primitive by Western tourist standards. A surprising amount of the old Romania survived Ceausescu's devastations, and the people welcome Western visitors and are usually delighted to practise their English. Intending visitors should check with others who have visited recently, to find out the current situation; and also with their local relief organisations to see if there is anything they can usefully deliver or carry while over there, such as medicine or other necessities. In any case, for a country so long largely isolated from Western visitors, the more who visit from the West and the stronger the links of friendship made, the better.